England the Country of my Birth - 2nd Edition

A pictorial and descriptive personal journey through the history of England the Country of the authors birth featuring amongst others an Iceni Queen, a Great British war hero and much, much more.

by Norfolk Watercolour Artist Alan R. Massen
Published in Great Britain by Rainbow Publications UK

First Published in 2016 by Rainbow Publications UK
2nd Edition Published in 2019 by Rainbow Publications UK

Copyright © 2019 Alan R. Massen

The moral right of Alan R. Massen to be identified as the author of this work has been asserted in accordance with the UK Copyright, Designs and Patents Act of 1988. - All rights reserved.

No part of this book may be reproduced, or stored in a retrieval system, or transmitted in any form or by any means, electronic, mechanical, photocopying, recording, or otherwise, without the prior written permission of both the author and the above publisher of this book All imagery and illustrations

© Alan R. Massen

Neither the publisher nor the author can accept liability for the use of any of the materials, methods or information recommended in this book or for any consequences arising out of their use, nor can they be held responsible for any errors or omissions that may be found in the text or may occur at a future date as a result of changes in rules, laws or equipment All manufacturers, sellers, product names and services identified in this book are used in editorial fashion and for the benefit of such companies with no intention of any infringement of trademarks. No such use or the use of any trade name is intended to convey endorsement or other affiliation with this book

Paperback Edition ISBN 978-0-9935591-0-5
Typeset in Minion Pro
Published in Great Britain by Rainbow Publications UK

About the Author

Alan was born in the city of Norwich in the county of Norfolk, England in November 1949. When Alan was still a teenager he started painting whilst attending art classes in Norwich. In his mid-teens he had two paintings accepted for a National Art Exhibition held in London and other major UK cities.

Alan spent most of his working life as a professional Health and Safety Advisor and rarely picked up a paint brush until Alan, his wife Susie and daughter Ginny (his other daughter Mandy is married and lives with her husband Adrian in Sheffield) moved out of the city of Norwich into the countryside in 1993. They moved to a little village called East Lexham in the heart of Norfolk. The village was very peaceful and pretty. This helped inspire Alan to take up watercolour painting once again.

In 2004 they moved to another small West Norfolk village near Downham Market where they still live today. In 2008 Alan had to retire due to ill health (bad knees) and whilst he still painted regularly he began to spend more and more time gardening. In 2013 his wife Susie suggested that he kept a gardening diary to record his adventures in the garden and capture the changing seasons, animals, birds and the successes and failures of being a gardener he encountered. By the following year Susie suggested that he should write a book from his diary and include illustrations of both the garden and his artwork.

In 2014 Alan's first book was published by Creative Gateway called **"Retiring to the Garden – Year One"**. This proved such a success that Alan decided to follow this up with his second book called **"Retiring into a Rainbow"** featuring his watercolour paintings. He then in 2015 published **"Retiring to Our Garden – Year Two"** published this time by Rainbow Publications UK. He then re-issued his first two books this time in a **"Second Edition"**. Also published by Rainbow Publications UK.

In 2016 he published: **"Skiathos a Greek Island Paradise", "Norfolk the County of my Birth", "Art Inspired by a Rainbow", "Ibiza Island of Dreams", "Majorca Island in the Sun", "Flip-flops and Shades on Thassos"** and finally **"Mardle and a Troshin' in Norfolk"**.

He has recently started on the following new books which will be entitled: **"England the Country of my Birth", "Mousehole the Cornish Jewel", "Sunshine and Shades on Kefalonia", "Shades and Flip-flops on Zakynthos", "Crete and the Island of Santorini", "Cyprus the Pyramids and the Holy Land", "Corfu and Mainland Greece" ", "Trips into my Mind's Eye"** and finally **"Flip-flops and Shades on many Greek Islands"**. When completed they will also be published by Rainbow Publications UK…

Books by the same Author

Retiring to the Garden – Year 1

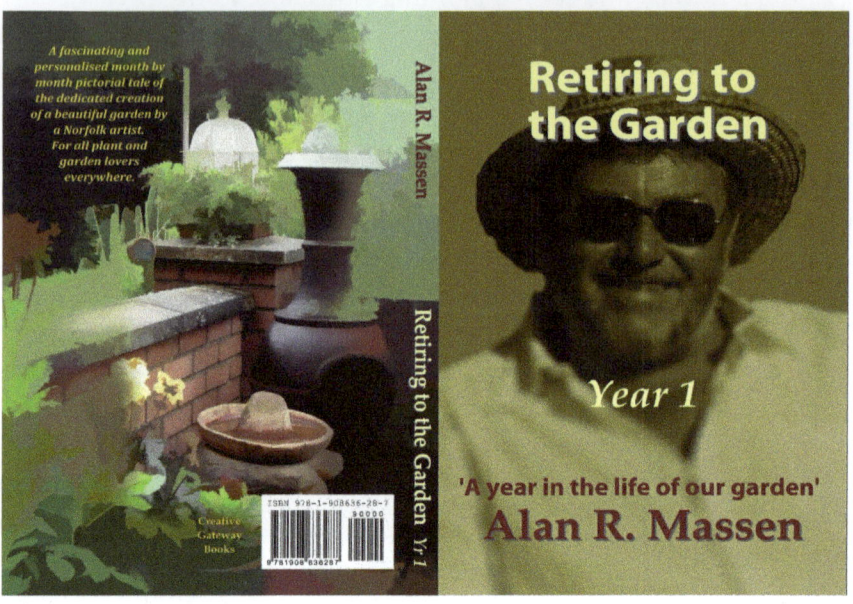

Retiring to Our Garden – Year 1 - 2nd Edition

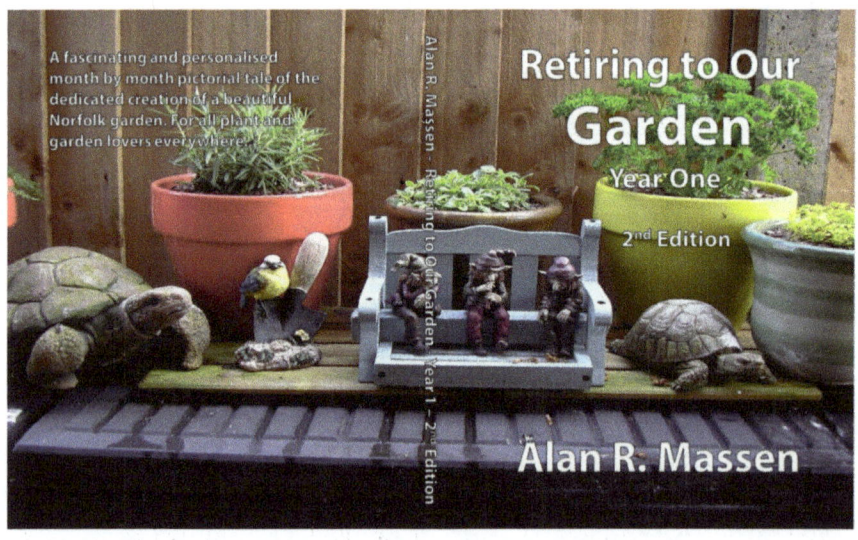

by Norfolk watercolour artist Alan R. Massen.
Published in Great Britain by Creative Gateway and Rainbow Publications UK

Books by the same Author

Retiring into a Rainbow - 2nd Edition

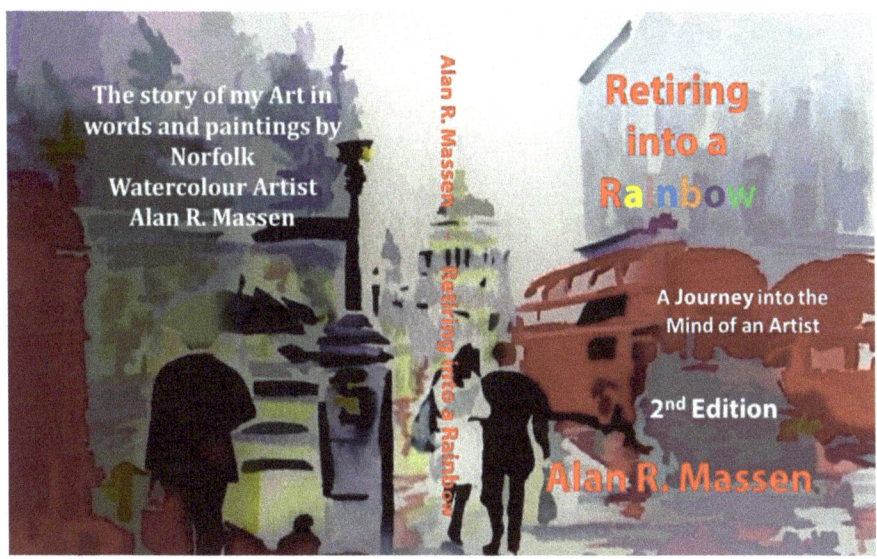

Retiring to Our Garden – Year Two

by Norfolk watercolour artist Alan R. Massen.
Published 1st Edition by Creative Gateway and 2nd Edition by Rainbow Publications UK

Books by the same Author

Skiathos a Greek Island Paradise

Norfolk the County of my Birth

by Norfolk watercolour artist Alan R. Massen.
Published in Great Britain by Rainbow Publications UK

Books by the same Author

Ibiza Island of Dreams

Majorca Island of the Sun

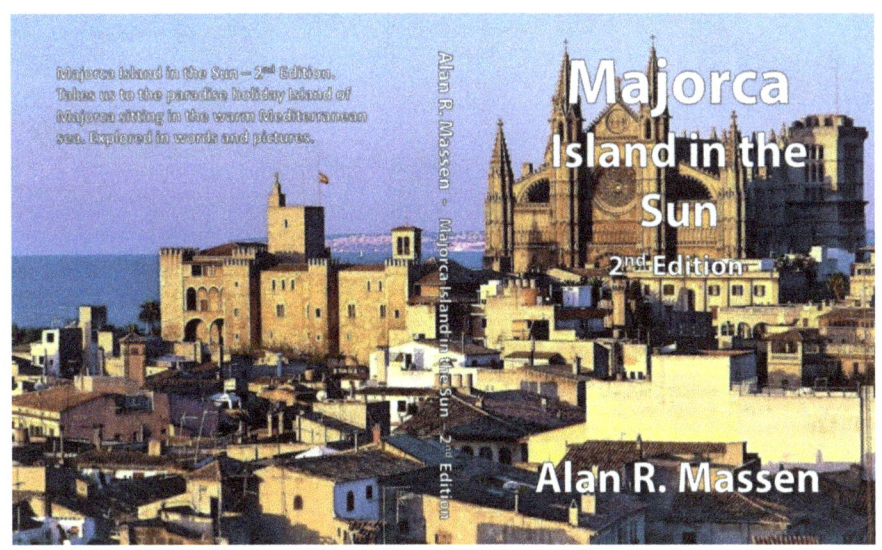

by Norfolk Watercolour Artist Alan R. Massen
Published in Great Britain by Rainbow Publications UK

Books by the same Author

Art Inspired by a Rainbow

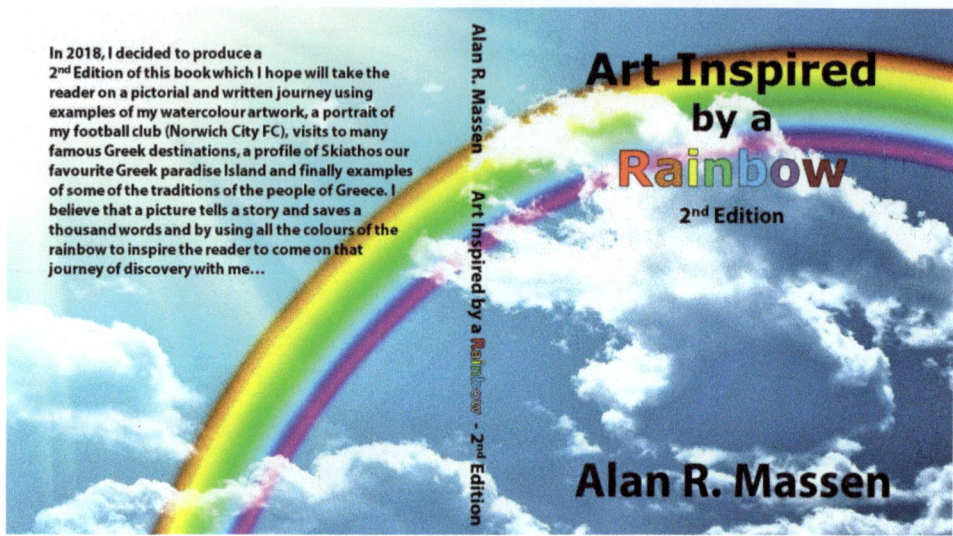

Flip-flops and Shades on Thassos

by Norfolk Watercolour Artist Alan R. Massen
Published in Great Britain by Rainbow Publications UK

Books by the same Author

Mardle and a Troshin' in Norfolk

Flip-flops and Shades on many Greek Islands

by Norfolk Watercolour Artist Alan R. Massen
Published in Great Britain by Rainbow Publications UK

Book by the same Author

England the Country of my Birth

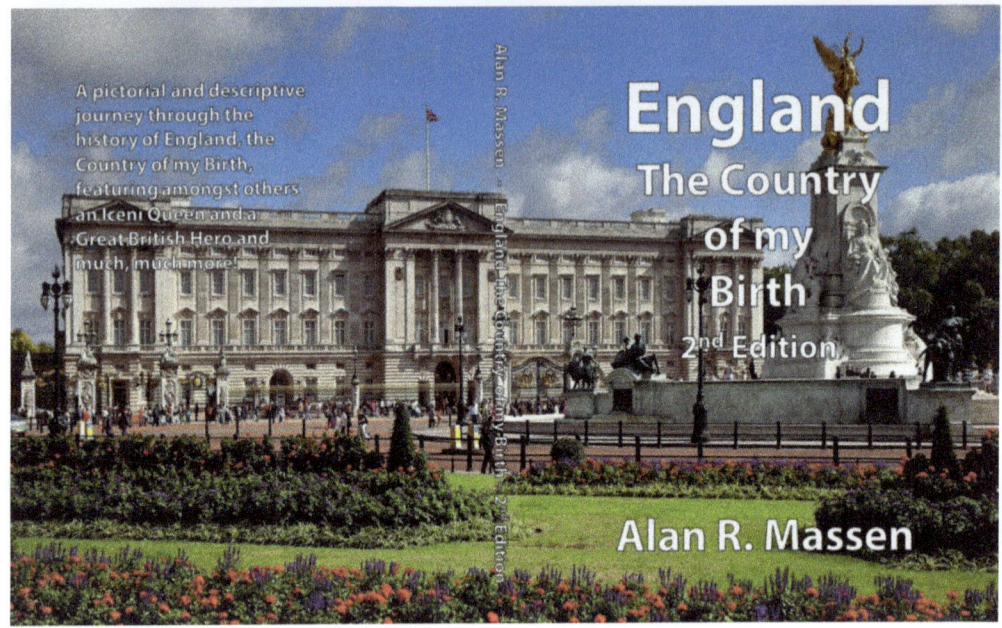

A pictorial and descriptive personal journey through the history of England the Country of the authors birth featuring amongst others an Iceni Queen, a Great British Hero and much, much more. Norfolk watercolour artist Alan R. Massen.

Also included in this book are artwork of the UK by Alan R. Massen
Published in Great Britain by Rainbow Publications UK

Book by the same Author

Mousehole the Cornish Jewel

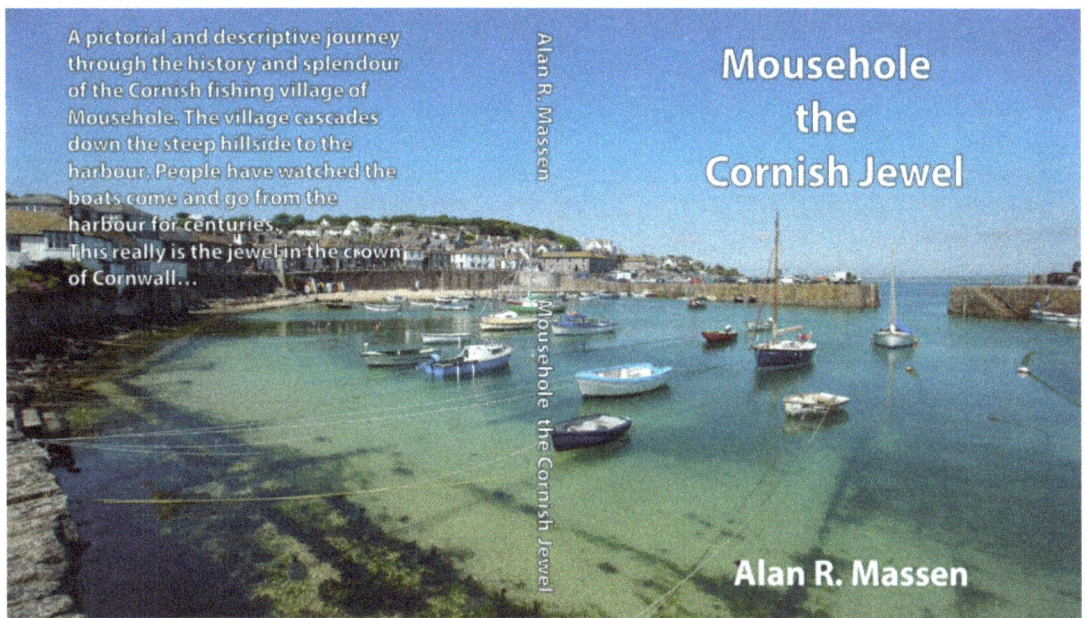

by Norfolk Watercolour Artist Alan R. Massen
Published in Great Britain by Rainbow Publications UK

Books by the same Author

Sunshine and Shades on Kefalonia

Shades and Flip-flops on Zakynthos

by Norfolk Watercolour Artist - Alan R. Massen
Published in Great Britain by Rainbow Publications UK

Books by the same Author

Crete and the Island of Santorini

Cyprus the Pyramids and the Holy Land

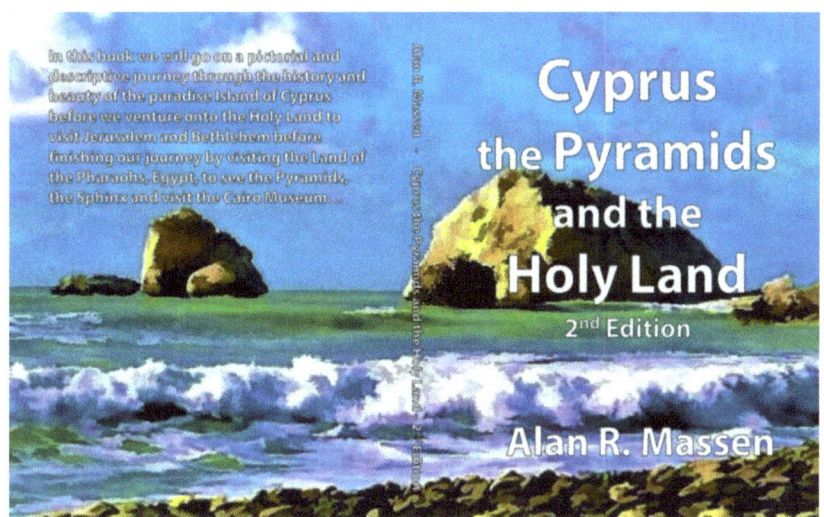

by Norfolk Watercolour Artist - Alan R. Massen
Published in Great Britain by Rainbow Publications UK

Books by the same Author

Trips into my Mind's Eye

Corfu and Mainland Greece

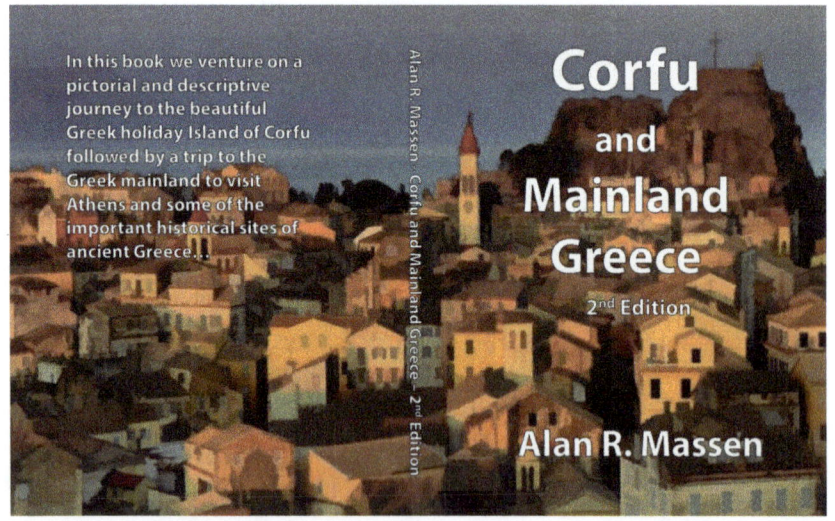

by Norfolk Watercolour Artist - Alan R. Massen
Published in Great Britain by Rainbow Publications UK

Dedication

I would like to dedicate this book to my football team Norwich City FC (the Canaries of Carrow Road, Norwich) who I have been supporting for more than sixty years. On Saturday 27th April 2019 Norwich City beat Blackburn Rovers 2 - 1 at home to guarantee promotion back to the Premier League next season. In November 2019 I will be seventy years of age and I am so proud and excited that my team will be playing, against the big boys, once more in the top division of English football league. On the Ball City - Come on you YELLOWS…

The Canary flying high and My Yellow and Green Champions

I would also like to dedicate this book to our friends Andy, Lynn, Alistair, Issy, Karl, Anna and finally a big thank you must go to the people of Great Britain who have in the past and who continue to help make this wonderful Green and Pleasant Land of Great Britain what it is today.

A special mention to my wife Susie who accompanies me and helps me to enjoy fully my life every single day in **"England the Country of my Birth"** and beyond.

I hope you will all enjoy this step back in time to try and find out who were the people that came before me and the distant roots of the country of my birth…

Contents

Introduction	1
The Stone Age	6
The Bronze Age	21
The Iron Age	34
Roman Britain	45
Anglo-Saxon Britain	59
Norman Britain	73
Tudor Britain	82
Stuart Britain	95
Geogian Britain	101
Victorian Britain	114
Edwardian Britain	130
The First World War	141
The Second World War	154
Post War Britain - Great Britain from 1945 to 2019	172
Acknowledgement	202

Copyright © 2019 Alan R. Massen

Introduction

Where do we come from?

In this my 14th book, that I have had published, we will be travelling back in time to discover the answer to that often asked question "where do I come from". This is a big question and in this book I will be looking at the country of my birth England and its history since time began to begin my journey of discovery to find my roots and the answer to the question above.

England flag and the flag of Great Britain.

Where do I come from?

In one of my other books I wrote about **"Norfolk the County of My Birth"** and by doing this it inspired me to find out more about **"England the Country of my Birth"**. In England we have the advantage of not just being English but also along with our friends from Scotland, Wales and Northern Ireland we also belong to the wider family of Great Britain and the Commonwealth beyond…

Introduction

When I started to research the history of Great Britain, before producing a draft of this book, it soon became apparent to me that I would need to spend a lot of time reading and researching this vast topic area, before I started to write this book. I found out that a TV programme called "Time Team", which was recorded over a twenty year period, was being repeated on afternoon TV. As I had enjoyed this archeologically based factual programme, in the past, I decided to watch it as part of my research. The programme, is introduced by Tony Robinson and featuring archaeologist Mick Ashley and Phil Harding and many other skilled contributors. I decided to spend some time watching the re-runs. So using reference books, Internet, watching Time Team and making copious notes I began to get a deeper understanding of my past and the events and people that have shaped who I am today. Having done this, what follows is my attempt at recording key milestones in our history from a personal perspective.

Alan in sunglasses…

We will begin our journey, by looking at the arrival of humans on the landmass, we now call the UK. We will look at some of the aspects of the Stone Age, Bronze Age and Iron Age Britain before moving into the modern era. I will be giving what is just my personal view of events during Roman Britain, Anglo-Saxon Britain, Norman Britain, Tudor and Stuart eras before the Georgian, Victorian era and the Edwardian era. We will conclude our journey together through the history of the island of my birth by looking at aspects of the First and Second World Wars before coming more up to date…

Introduction

Throughout this book you will see examples of my watercolour paintings and pictorial artworks which I have produced on my computer, using a piece of art software, to give the pictures an impressionist style alongside the text. Although many of the illustrations used are of people, places animals and other things associated with England they may not necessarily add value to the text information. I have included these to give the reader some light relief from the academic nature of the text content. History could be seen by many as a dry subject but I have not found this to be true. I have found it to be very interesting, captivating and it has given me a greater sense of who I am.

Flags of Countries of the EU

I have tried to tell the story of the coming of man and woman to our shores and how their lives changed and developed over time. Including the inevitable influence of many other peoples coming from abroad, over time, to make a life and shape the country that I call my own. I have focused on the aspects of our past history that interest me personally and invite the reader to undertake further research into any aspects not covered in sufficient detail for them…

Introduction

Archaeologists:

I have always been very interested in our pasts and it is with thanks to such programmes as "Time Team" and others that have raised the profile of history and given us a much more detailed insight into our pasts.

The UK Flag and Coal Miners

In the watercolour above, we see miners waiting to go down the pit to dig the black stuff. It is just one of the patriotic images that can invoke, encourage and/or demonstrate peoples pride in the nation of their birth. We all have images that bring these feelings of pride to the fore. It could be the national flag, anthem or simply being in the beautiful landscape we call home…

Introduction

As we will discover in the pages that follow many different cultural and ethnic groups have immigrated to Great Britain since the history of this Island began.

This influx has made us what we are today and we owe this mix a great debt for leaving their legacy of religions, buildings, artefacts, books, artwork, skills and most of all a family tree that's leads directly from these distant peoples to us.

Red poppies…

Commonwealth soldiers

In recent years, as demonstrated by the image above, the people of Great Britain have been joined by all the peoples of the Commonwealth with Queen Elizabeth II, as the head of state for all these nations, that were formerly part of the British Empire. As they march away let us begin our journey to meet our ancestors by starting in the Stone Age…

The Stone Age

The Palaeolithic and Mesolithic, also known as the Old and Middle Stones Ages, were characterised by a hunter-gatherer economy and was a stone tool society.

When archaeologists today discover Stone Age flint tools that they used help demonstrate the high level of skills required in the production of such effective tools. Stone Age men and women were cleaver and just like us they used their brain and high levels of skills to survive and solve everyday problems allowing them to develop and prosper so long ago…

The Stone Age

Early Stone Age Man 400,000 BC:

When looking for the first signs of humans living in Britain I remember a Time Team programme that went to Elvedon in Suffolk, which is not very far away from where we live in Norfolk, there they found evidence of the earliest man on what is now known as the UK. Time Team investigated one of the very few places in Britain which shows evidence of human habitation dating from the early Stone Age. They excavated Stone Age flint tools and small flint chipping's that had been dropped on the edge of a river bank dating back to 400.000 BC.

What most of England would've looked like 400 millennia ago to the small Stone Age population who lived here is lots of lush vegetation, and plenty of animal life including lions, rhinos and elephants and contrary to what you see in the movies, definitely no dinosaurs. These early Stone Age men and women were hunter gathers and mainly lived on fruit, nuts, fish, shell fish and meat. So it is thanks to the Time Team and other archaeologists that we now know so much about our early forefathers…

The Stone Age

Early Stone Age Man 400,000 BC: These early settlers into Britain were skilled flint stone workers and made all the tools and weapons they needed out of this valued material:

At Elvedon near Thetford Norfolk, Time Team, discovered that 400,000 BC man had sat beside a river and using flint from the bank and river bed that they made their tools and weapons for hunting…

The Stone Age

Early Stone Age Man 400,000 BC:

Just a few miles away from Elvedon is Crimes Graves where Stone Age man later extracted high quality flint from mines in Norfolk (see below).

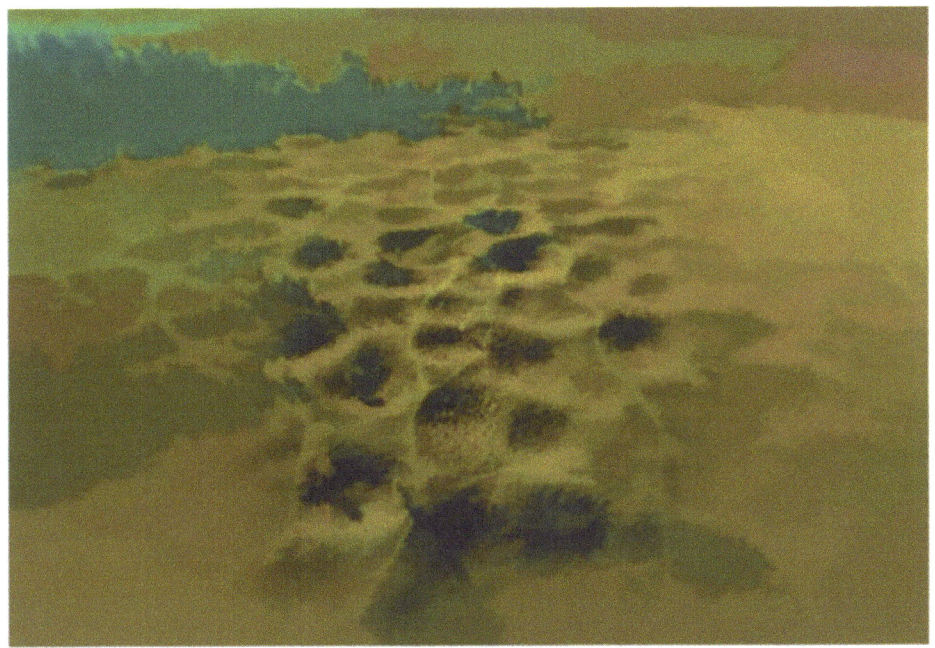

Grime's Graves is a large flint mining complex in Norfolk. It was worked between circa 3000 BC and circa 1900 BC, although production may have continued well into the Bronze and Iron Ages…

The Stone Age

The Lower Palaeolithic:

The Lower Palaeolithic period in Britain saw its first inhabitation by early hominids. One of the most prominent archaeological sites dating to this period is that of Boxgrove Quarry in West Sussex, southern England. By the Mesolithic period, Homo Sapiens, or modern humans, were the only hominid species to still survive in the British Isles…

The Stone Age

Middle Palaeolithic:

This period is best known as the era during which the Neanderthals lived in Europe and the Near East (c. 300,000–28,000 years ago). There is no evidence for Neanderthals in Africa, Australia or the Americas. Neanderthals nursed their elderly and practised ritual burial indicating an organised society.

Upper Paleolithic Early Stone Age:

This era is from 50,000 to 10,000 years ago in Europe. The Upper Palaeolithic is marked by a relatively rapid succession of often complex stone artefact technologies and a large increase in the creation of art and personal ornamentation…

The Stone Age

Mesolithic Middle Stone Age:

By the Mesolithic period, Homo Sapiens, or modern humans, were the only hominid species to still survive in the British Isles. The period starting from the end of the last ice age, 10,000 years ago, to around 6,000 years ago was characterized by rising sea levels and a need to adapt to a changing environment and find new food sources such as fruit and nuts.

This era saw the continued development of stone tools hence the term the Middle Stone Age…

The Stone Age

This was the time that man would manufacture more efficient composite tools, resulting in an intensification of hunting and fishing. There was also increasing social activity and the development of more complex settlements.

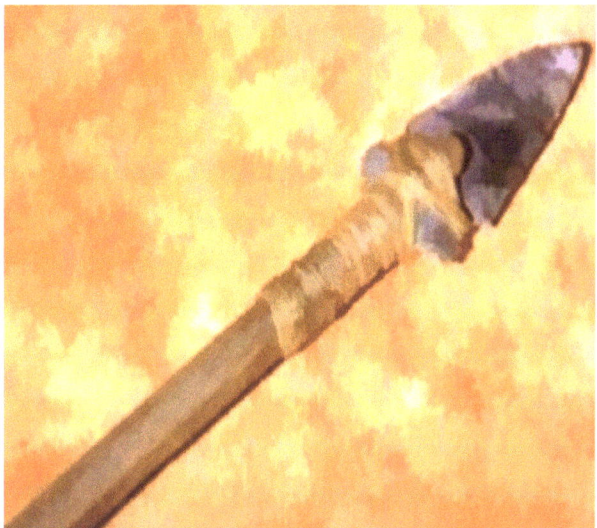

Domestication of the dog as a hunting companion probably dates to this period and this relationship has endured right up to the present day…

The Stone Age

The Neolithic, New Stone Age:

The Neolithic, New Stone Age, was approximately characterised by the adoption of agriculture, the shift from food gathering to food producing. In itself it is one of the most revolutionary changes in human history, so-called the Neolithic Revolution and the development of pottery, polished stone tools and more complex, larger settlements. Due to the increased need to harvest and process plants, ground stone and polished stone artefacts became much more widespread, including tools for grinding, cutting, and chopping...

The Stone Age

The first large-scale constructions were built at this time, including settlement towers and walls. The earliest evidence for established trade exists in the Neolithic period with newly settled people importing exotic goods over distances of many hundreds of miles. These facts show that there were sufficient resources and co-operation to enable large groups to work on these projects. After a summary of the Stone Age and some pictures depicting the Stone Age era before we move into the Bronze Age…

The Stone Age

Stone Age man

Summary of the Stone Age

The Stone Age was a time thousands of years ago, when early humans lived in caves and jungles. Life was simple, and there were only two main things to do, which were to protect themselves from the wild animals, and to gather food. It started almost with the evolution of mankind. For both purposes, early people made tools from flint stone. The oldest stone tool that we have as evidence is almost 3.4 million years old. It was found in Lower Awash Valley in Ethiopia. Stones were also used to make fire. And since in those times humans used stone for almost everything they did, we call it the Stone Age. The Stone Age ended somewhere in between 6000 BC to 2500 BC; around this time stone tools were replaced by tools made of copper…

The Stone Age

Summary of the Stone Age

In the early years of the Stone Age, humans used stone, wood and bone tools for chopping tasks. Later, they learnt to develop a special kind of sharp stone called flint which was used to cut and chip things quickly. They managed to get a very sharp edge ideal for cutting by napping the flint and became masters of this skill. As the humans became smarter they started to make even more complex tools than before. Flint chipping's were probably used as barbs on arrows, spears and other composite tools. The Stone Age people, at this time, just ate animals and plants. They wrapped themselves in animal fur and sat around a fire to keep warm. Stone Age people could communicate to each other with written symbols. All their words and ideas were expressed in symbols. They were talented artists. The Stone Age went on for a long time. Obviously in the beginning of the Stone Age rock shelters were the way to go. Any signs of trouble and the humans would go and hide in their caves…

The Stone Age

Summary of the Stone Age

In India, the Bhimbetka rock shelters show the earliest signs of human life in the region. They are almost 30,000 years old. Some researchers have discovered Stone Age art in European caves. The inside walls of the cave are adorned with realistic paintings of animals like horses, deer, and the woolly mammoth! In time the Stone Age humans moved out of their rock shelters because they wanted to live near water sources in the valleys. This was the time when, for the first time, humans kept dogs as pets and helpers. The last stage of the Stone Age was when people discovered farming and life became more systematic. Pots and pans were made out of clay. Large scale buildings were built. Stone walls with a straw roof were now common…

The Stone Age

A stone circle from the Stone Age

Stone Age man preparing to make colour for a rock Painting

The Stone Age

Stone Age village in the marshes

Stonehenge

The Bronze Age

In Great Britain, the Bronze Age is considered to have been the period from around 2100 BC to 750 BC.

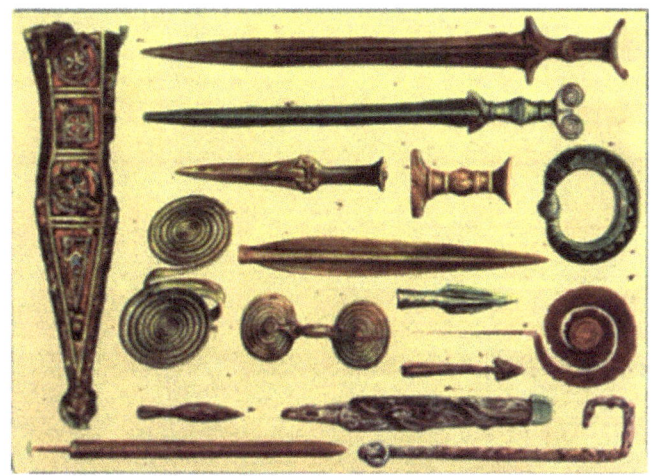

Moulds for casting bronze

During the Bronze Age period migration brought new people to the islands of Great Britain from the continent. Recent tooth enamel isotope research on bodies found in early Bronze Age graves around Stonehenge indicate that at least some of the migrants came from the area of modern day Switzerland…

The Bronze Age

At some point the Beaker people arrived from the Mediterranean into Great Britain. The Beaker culture displayed different behaviours from the earlier Neolithic people, and cultural change was significant. Integration is thought to have been peaceful, as many of the early henge sites were seemingly adopted by the newcomers.

Bronze Age round house under construction

A rich Wessex culture developed in southern Britain at this time. Additionally, the climate was deteriorating; where once the weather was warm and dry it became much wetter as the Bronze Age continued, forcing the population away from easily defended sites in the hills and into the fertile valleys…

The Bronze Age

Making bronze

Large livestock farms developed in the lowlands and appear to have contributed to economic growth and inspired increasing forest clearances. The Deverel-Rimbury culture began to emerge in the second half of the Middle Bronze Age (c. 1400–1100 BC) to exploit these conditions. Devon and Cornwall were major sources of tin for much of Western Europe and copper was extracted from sites such as the Great Orme mine in northern Wales. These rich resources were then traded with people from far and wide…

The Bronze Age

Social groups appear to have been tribal but with growing complexity and hierarchies becoming apparent. The burial of the dead (which, until this period, had usually been communal) became much more individual in nature.

Bronze Age burial

In the Neolithic period it was the usual practice for a large chambered cairn or long barrow to be used to house the dead. In the Early Bronze Age people however, buried their dead, in individual barrows or sometimes in cists covered with cairns.

In Bronze Age Britain people lived in small family homesteads of roundhouses…

The Bronze Age

The greatest quantities of bronze objects found in England were discovered in the county of Cambridgeshire, where the most important finds were recovered at a place called Isleham. In this period the alloying of copper with zinc or tin to make brass or bronze was developed and practised soon after the discovery of copper itself. Today science has established through carbon dating that mining commenced at around 2280 BC to 1890 BC…

The Bronze Age

A Bronze Age farmer and a round house settlement

In the British Isles, the Neolithic and Bronze Ages saw the transformation of British and Irish society and landscape with the introduction of improved building, tool making and land cultivation. This was the time when man first began to live much as we do today. It saw the adoption of agriculture, as communities gave up their hunter-gatherer modes of existence to begin farming. They were now living in wooden round houses roofed with reeds or straw. Just before we see how man developed his metal working skills in the Iron Age we will have a summary of the Bronze Age and some more pictures…

The Bronze Age

A Bronze Age shield

Summary of the Bronze Age

The beginning of the Bronze Age in Britain can be put at around 2,000 BC. Although this is not certain, it is generally thought that the new bronze tools and weapons identified with this age were brought over from continental Europe. The skulls recovered from burial sites from the Bronze Age are different in shape from Stone Age skulls. This would suggest that new ideas and new blood were brought over from the continent. Stone and bronze can and were used by the local population together, subject to the availability of both materials. True bronze is a combination of 10% tin and 90% copper. Both materials were readily available in Britain at this time. Before its entry into Britain, the Bronze Age was in full swing in Europe. The island of Crete was the centre for the expansion of the bronze trade to Europe and people migrated from there to other places in Europe as well as into Great Britain…

The Bronze Age

Bronze Age round house

Summary of the Bronze Age

The Beaker people:

It is widely thought, although not certain, that bronze was first brought over to Britain by the Bell Beaker folk. The local people were living in round houses at the time (see above) and these soon became home to the incoming Beaker people as well. The Beaker people were so named because of their distinctive bell-shaped pottery drinking vessels. They probably came up through the south-west coast of Britain, which at the time had rich deposits of copper and tin so this area was attractive to Europeans. The Bell Beaker folk readily mixed with any new culture they encountered, including the Neolithic farmers they found in Britain, and Bell Beaker pottery has been found in megalithic tombs and temples dated back to this time…

The Bronze Age

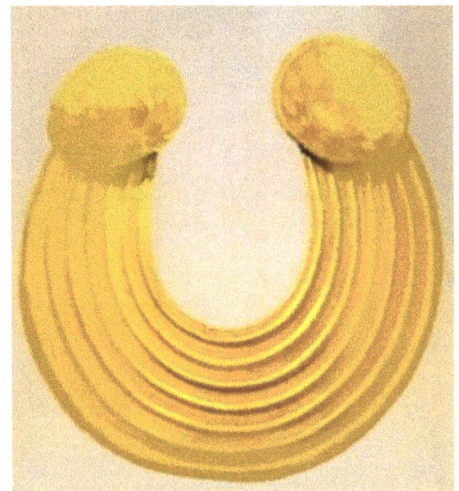

Bronze Age round house and a gold torts

Summary of the Bronze Age

The Beaker people:

The Beaker people improved the existing temple at Stonehenge, which is good proof that they got on well with the original inhabitants. At Avebury, close by, they constructed another great henge monument. Avebury has a large circular ditch and bank, and within it was a ring of standing stones. Unfortunately today the standings stones have now all gone. Nearby, at Silbury Hill, stands the largest man-made mound in prehistoric Britain, again thought to have been made by the Beaker people however, no burial has been found inside it…

The Bronze Age

A Bronze Age hunting party

Summary of the Bronze Age

The Beaker people:

The emergence of the Beaker people in Britain gave rise to what is now termed the Wessex Culture. This is the name given to a number of very rich grave goods found under round barrows in southern Britain. The grave goods include well-made stone battle axes, metal daggers with elaborately decorated hilts, and precious ornaments of gold and amber. The finds are some of the loveliest prehistoric objects ever to be found in Great Britain. Among the golden cups found in the graves, some were found that were so like those of the Mycenae that they are used as examples to prove the existence of trade between Wessex and Greece. It is great to think that people travel to and from Great Britain all those years ago and today many people, Susie and I included, travel from Great Britain to and back from the Greek Islands for their summer holidays. This shows that such exchanges of goods and services are not a new thing but date back to the very beginning of the modern era…

The Bronze Age

The Bronze Age Sea Henge recently found on a Norfolk beach

Summary of the Bronze Age

The later Bronze Age:

Textile production had also got under way by this time. Women would wear long woollen skirts and short tunics. The men wore knee-length wrap-around skirts, or kilt-like woolens, as well as tunics, cloaks and even one-piece garments. The men were also clean-shaven, long-haired and wore round woollen hats. The standard farming household consisted of two houses, a main living house and second structure used for cooking and textile production. The dead, of this period, were cremated, and buried in small cemeteries behind each settlement. The large burial sites of the early Bronze Age were a thing of the past, as the land was now needed for agriculture…

The Bronze Age

Bronze Age jewellery

Summary of the Bronze Age

The later Bronze Age:

The late Bronze Age was also a time of advanced pottery-making techniques, and more sophisticated weapon-making. The making and wearing of stunning jewellery was also taking place during this period. The Iron Age that followed it did not happen suddenly, but is thought to have started in Britain around 650 BC and finished around AD 43. Again, the knowledge of iron-making was brought to Britain by Europeans, who had already started to build the first blast furnaces. To sum up, the period of Bronze Age man had lasted for almost 1,500 years. At the end of this era the people took the giant step from the Stone Age into the Iron Age and the beginning of the modern era…

The Bronze Age

Inside a Bronze Age round house

Music making in a Bronze Age round house

The Iron Age

The British Iron Age is the conventional name used in Great Britain which refers to both the prehistoric and the early centuries AD phases of the Iron Age culture of the mainland of Great Britain and its smaller islands. The British Iron Age lasted in theory from the first significant use of iron for tools and weapons in Britain to the coming of the Romans to the southern half of the island. The Brythonic languages were spoken in Great Britain at this time, as well as others including the Goidelic and Gaulish languages of neighbouring Ireland and Gaul respectively…

The Iron Age

The British Iron Age is also characterised by the adoption of iron, a metal which was used to produce a variety of different tools, ornaments and weapons. In the course of the first millennium BC, immigration from continental Europe resulted in the establishment of Celtic languages in the islands of Great Britain. Near the end of the Iron Age Britain was invaded by the Romans who established a Romanised culture in the areas they controlled and that is where we are heading next after a summary of this period and viewing some more Iron Age pictures…

The Iron Age

Iron Age Man

Summary of the Iron Age

The period known as the Iron Age lasted in Britain for about 800 years (from 750 BC to AD 43). The changes and technological innovations that occurred during this time were every bit as evolutionary as those that have occurred in the last 800 years, from the 13th century to the present day. By the end of the Iron Age, amongst other things, coinage had been introduced, wheel thrown pottery was being made, there was an increased interest in personal appearance, people had started to live in larger and more settled communities, and the mortuary rites of society had changed. Furthermore, because of climatic, geographical and topographical differences, someone living in Yorkshire or Ireland would have eaten different food, worn different clothing and lived in different housing conditions from someone living in southern Britain. Due to these ranges, and the varying evidence of the archaeology, the pattern of everyday life in an Iron Age village has to be described in quite generalised terms…

The Iron Age

An Iron Age round house

Summary of the Iron Age

Iron Age Agriculture:

The Iron Age society was primarily based around agricultural, it is safe to presume that the daily routine would have revolved around the maintenance of the crops and livestock. Small farmsteads were tended by, and would have supported, isolated communities of family or extended family size, producing enough to live on and a little extra to exchange for commodities that the farmers were unable to provide for themselves. Many of these small farmsteads, such as at Farley Mount in Hampshire, delimited with a circular bank and ditch enclosure, were surrounded by linear ditch systems that formed small rectangular fields, radiating out from the farm itself. Environmental evidence, in the form of carbonised grains and pollen, has shown that new crops such as emmer wheat were introduced, in addition to the spelt wheat, barley, rye and oats already grown in these fields. Harvested crops were stored in either granaries that were raised from the ground on posts, or in bell-shaped pits 2-3 m (6-7 ft) deep, dug into the chalk landscape. Some 4,500 of these storage pits have been found within the hillfort interior at Danebury in Hampshire, and if they were all used to store crops, this would have essentially made the site one large fortified granary…

The Iron Age

Iron Age man and his dog

Summary of the Iron Age

Iron Age Livestock:

Although cattle and sheep would have been the most common farm animals, it is known that pigs were also kept. The animals would have aided the family, not only with heavy farm labour, in the case of the cattle, such as the ploughing of crop fields, but also as a valuable form of manure, wool or hide, and food products. Horses and dogs are also observed in the archaeological evidence from both faunal remains and artefacts. Horses were used for pulling 2 or 4 wheeled vehicles (carts, chariots), while dogs would have assisted in the herding of the livestock and hunting…

The Iron Age

Iron Age man taming the wild animals to use on the land

Iron Age round houses

Summary of the Iron Age

Iron Age Lifestyle:

A very well preserved settlement has been discovered at the site of Chysauster in Cornwall. It was made up of individual houses of stone with garden plots, clustered along a street. In central southern Britain in about the sixth century, hill-forts with large bank and ditch enclosures in prominent positions in the landscape were starting to be built. The archaeological evidence shows that the enclosures were densely occupied, with circular houses and roads. In Wessex, the typical building on a settlement would have been the large roundhouse. All of the domestic life would have occurred within this…

The Iron Age

An Iron Age settlement

Summary of the Iron Age

The Iron Age Roundhouse:
The main frame of an Iron Age roundhouse would have been made of upright timbers, which were interwoven with coppiced wood. This was usually hazel, oak, ash or pollarded willow, to make wattle walls. This was then covered with a daub made from clay, soil, straw and animal manure that would weatherproof the house. The roof was constructed from large timbers and was densely thatched. The main focus of the interior of the house was the central open-hearth fire. This was the heart of the house and an indispensable feature that provided cooked food, warmth and light. Because of its importance within the domestic sphere, the fire would have been maintained 24 hours a day. Beside the fire may have stood a pair of firedogs or suspended above it a bronze cauldron held up by a tripod and it was attached to this by an adjustable chain…

The Iron Age

The Iron Age Roundhouse settlement fort

Summary of the Iron Age

The ordinary basic cooking pots would have been made by hand, from the local clay and came in varying rounded shapes, occasionally with simple incised decoration. As for eating, bread would have been an important part of any meal, and was made from wheat and barley ground down into flour using a quern-stone. The dough would have then been baked in a simple clay-domed oven, of which evidence has been found in Iron Age roundhouses. The barley and rye could also have been made into a kind of porridge, evidence for which has been found in the stomach contents in preserved Iron Age bodies that have been deposited in peat bogs in northern Europe. In addition to this, the Roman writer Pliny explains that grain was also fermented to make beer, and the surface foam that formed was scraped off and used in the bread-making process. Other than cereal grains, few plant materials have survived. However we can assume that Iron Age people supplemented their diet with edible berries, leaves, flowers, nuts and roots. The animals reared as livestock, pigs, cattle and sheep, would have been eaten. Milk and dairy products would have been available in addition to fish, birds, and the occasional wild animal. The evidence of beeswax in the bronze-casting techniques shows that honey would also have been available as a sweetener. The interior of the house was an ideal place for the drying and preservation of food. Smoke and heat from the constantly maintained fire would have smoked meat and fish, and would have dried herbs and other plants perfectly. Salt was another means of preserving meat for the cold winter months, but this was a commodity that could not be made at a typical settlement it had to be obtained by using bartering trade…

The Iron Age

Iron Age pots

Summary of the Iron Age

Leisure time in an Iron Age Roundhouse:

In another part of the roundhouse would have been an upright weaving loom. The wool from the sheep was spun and woven to make clothes. Spindle-whorls (round clay/stone weights used to make the spindle rotate evenly), carved bone weaving combs, and loom weights also of stone or clay, which held down the warp threads on the loom, are found on many Iron Age domestic sites. At the end of the day, having tended to the livestock, there would presumably, have been time to rest. This may have been a matter of sitting by the fire on logs, drinking freshly brewed beer from a drinking horn made of antler and talking to the other members of the house. As for leisure activities for both the young and old, glass gaming pieces have been found in some of the later Iron Age burials, showing that forms of board games may have been available. Children, who during the day would have helped in the house, or tended livestock, may have occupied their free time by practising their skill at the slingshot which was a common and accessible weapon in the Iron Age…

The Iron Age

Leaving an Iron Age hill fort…

Summary of the Iron Age

The Iron Age Roundhouse sleeping arrangements:

On one side of the roundhouse's interior, and based on internal post-holes, would have been the sleeping quarters. These bed areas may have been raised from the ground on a wooden base; with hay or feather mattresses, strewn with animal skins and wool blankets. The thick thatch of the roof and the constant heat from the fire would have made the interior of the roundhouse quite a snug and comfortable place to live in.

Iron Age clothing:

Our understanding of how people dressed and cared for their appearance has come partly from the archaeological evidence, but mainly from what classical writers such as Strabo and Diodorus Siculus wrote, amazed at the difference from the plain coloured togas that they were used to. One of the main differences was that Britain's Iron Age people are said to have worn a form of close-fitting trousers (braccae), with a long tunic of either linen or wool, held at the waist with a belt. Over this would have been a cloak that was fastened at the shoulder with a brooch. The textiles were dyed bright colours and were woven with striped or checked patterns. There is evidence from the archaeological record of brooches, pins and other dress accessories that would have played both a functional and decorative role on the clothing. The classical texts mention that both women and men may have grown their hair long, sometimes plaited, and that the men sported either beards or moustaches, which they also grew long…

The Iron Age

Summary of the Iron Age

Iron Age religion and ritual:

It is thought that since farming played such an important role in the Iron Age community, the religious festivals would have followed the same seasonal pattern, based around the agricultural year. There is evidence from sites such as Winnall Down and Danebury in Hampshire that some pits are filled with specially chosen 'offerings', such as animal carcasses and even human remains. These special deposits may have been the result of rituals or ceremonies, including feasts, possibly from these seasonal festivals. The Iron Age was still in full flow when the Romans invaded the shores of Britain.

British Iron Age men preparing for war with the Romans

As we draw towards the end of the Iron Age the need to practice the art of combat became more and more important. Across the sea a gathering of the might of the Roman Army waited just across the channel which meant that it was only a matter of time before they would crossed and marched into what was to become Roman Britain…

Roman Britain

Roman Britain: Classical period (AD 40 – AD 410):

The Roman army arrives in Great Britain

From AD 40 to about AD 410, southern Britain was part of the Roman Empire. Julius Caesar invaded Britain in both 54 BC and again in 55 BC as part of his Gallic Wars. This was because the Britons had been overrun or culturally assimilated by other Celtic tribes during the British Iron Age and had been providing aid to Caesar's enemies. The Emperor Julius Caesar received tribute, installed a friendly King over the Trinovantes and then returned to Gaul. Planned invasions under Augustus were called off in 34 BC, 27 BC, and 25 BC…

Roman Britain

In 40 AD, Caligula assembled more than 200,000 men at the Channel only to have them gather seashells. Three years later, Claudius directed four legions to invade Britain. The Romans defeated the Catuvellauni and then organised their conquests as the Province of Britain (Latin: Provincia Britannia). By the year 47, the Romans held the lands southeast of the Fosse Way. They were to remain in Britain for many more years to come …

Roman Britain

Queen Boudica of the Norfolk Iceni Tribe

A Norfolk Hero

The Norfolk hero Queen Boudica was a local Norfolk chieftain who fought and almost defeated the mighty Roman Army, way back in the first century A.D. Her tribe the Iceni lived in what we now call Norfolk In my watercolour painting (above), I tried to endow a sense of how I think she would have looked. She is reputed to have had red hair and wore a blue dye called woad on her face to make her more frightening to her enemies. She lived just up the road from where we live today. She was married to King Prasutagus and upon his death she was flogged by the Romans who she then went on to fight until her death in AD 61. Boudica is another great example of the important role females have played in all of history and how with determination, pride and other warrior traits, even a gentle woman can make a fearsome opponent…

Roman Britain

Because of the Boudica rebellion Roman control over Wales was delayed but the Romans expanded steadily northward and two walls were built later called Hadrian's wall to defend the Roman province from the Caledonians, thus the realms in the Scottish Highlands were never directly controlled.

Roman soldiers battle ready…

Hadrian and his wall

The Romans introduced coinage, new religions proper surfaced roads, stone built villas and even bath houses amongst other important civilisation steps forward…

Roman Britain

As Roman itself began its decline and for much of the later period of the Roman occupation of Great Britain, Britannia was subject to barbarian invasions and often came under the control of imperial usurpers and Imperial pretenders.

The barbarians at the walls of Rome

The final withdrawal from Britain was made in around 410 AD, after which the native Kingdoms are considered to have formed post Roman Britain…

Roman Britain

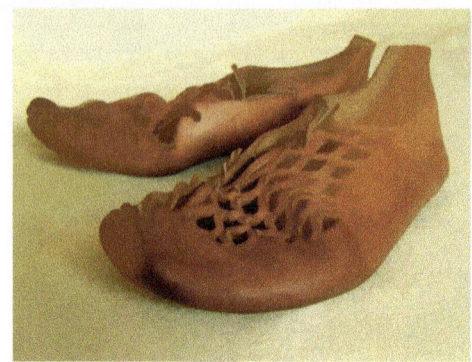

A Roman soldiers helmet, sandals and a Roman officer and his men

The Roman occupation unquestionably had an effect on Britain, but it is easy to overstate how widespread the effect was. Although the form of life changed for some people, the essence of Britain Celtic society was altered very little. The Roman classical writer Strabo actually comments that Britain was famed for its hunting dogs, which were exported throughout the Roman Empire.

The Administration of Roman Britain

One of the first things the Romans did was to involve the conquered tribes in the administration of the province. They set up administrative areas according to traditional tribal territories, and involved the tribal aristocracies in the decision making process. This was standard Roman practice, and a wise one. They made the conquered people responsible for their own administration within a Roman framework. It was part of their plan to bring the benefits of civilisation, Roman style, to other peoples. It worked, for the way to prestige and social advancement was through the Roman bureaucracy…

Roman Britain

Roman fort on mainland Britain

Summary of Roman Britain

Towns in Roman Britain:

The Romans in Britain encouraged the growth of towns. The Romans saw urban life as the epitome of sophisticated civilization. They encouraged the growth of towns near their army bases, and established special towns as settlements for retired soldiers. They encouraged the ruling class of Celtic aristocrats to build town dwellings, and they made the towns the location of vibrant commercial activity. As elsewhere in the Empire, the local "councils" in the towns were encouraged to build civic buildings as a mark of civilization. The Romans built towns in lowland areas, such as at fords across rivers, in contrast to the earlier Neolithic and Iron Age practice of sticking to the slopes and higher ground above the valleys. Town boundaries, unlike military forts, were not laid out in rigid rectangles or squares, but they did contain a regular grid-like network of streets. Most towns were walled, though at first the walls would have been no more than earthen banks with ditches. By the 3rd and certainly by the 4th century the earthen banks were replaced by stone and masonry…

Roman Britain

Summary of Roman Britain

Towns in Roman Britain: At the centre of a Roman town was a forum, or civic centre. Usually an open square or rectangle with colonnades, the forum gave access to the basilica, or town hall. It was here that courts of justice were held, though it could also be used as a place for merchants to assemble. Town life was a real social revolution for the largely rural Celtic society. Those who aspired to the wealth and prosperity that came with the Roman occupation threw themselves into life in the towns.

Public Baths in Roman Britain Towns: Every town had public baths. The baths were a Roman institution, and most town dwellers would have attended daily before their evening meal. They were open to both sexes, though at different times of day, and served as a combination health club, healing spa, and meeting place. The order that people went through the baths seems to have been up to the individual, though they were generally arranged in the order of exercise area, disrobing area, cold room, warm room, and hot rooms. Some baths further divided up the hot rooms into steam and dry heat areas…

Roman Britain

A Roman Britain farm

Summary of Roman Britain

Entertainment for the public in Roman Britain Towns:

Many towns also offered the entertainments of the theatre and amphitheatre. The theatre, an open air tiered clam-shell, would have offered fare from classical plays, pantomime and religious festivals. The amphitheatre, an open air oval, would have appealed to a less discriminating taste, offering gladiatorial combats, contests between men and animals, and public executions. The number of theatres and amphitheatres in Britain is small, so these particular entertainments may not have been so popular.

Roads in Roman Britain:

Joining the towns together were the Roman roads. Over the course of the occupation the Romans built over 9600 km's of roads in Britain. Although, contrary to reputation, they weren't always straight, they were amazingly well built, and made troop movement and later the movement of commercial goods much easier. The imperial posting service, used by Roman officials, maintained inns and relays of horses and were kept, at intervals of 30 to 50 km along the roads. The roads were literally highways, raised up on a cambered bank of material dug from roadside ditches. They were constructed in several layers, the final layer generally being gravel or flint, and from 4 to 8 meters wide…

Roman Britain

A horde of Roman coins

Summary of Roman Britain

Villas in Roman Britain:

Aside from the towns, the other sign of Romanised civilization was the growth of villas. In Latin the word villa means simply, "farm", so technically villas were any form of rural agricultural dwelling built in a Roman style. In practice, though, when we speak of villas we mean the country estates of the Romanised British elite. Although at first the conquered tribal aristocracy may have been drawn into towns, it wasn't long before they began a "back to the land" movement. Most large villas are built quite close to major urban centres, generally within ten miles, so the owners were never very far from the centre of affairs. Villas were more than fancy houses, though; they were centres of rural industry and agriculture. In one complex they could hold the landowner and his family, overseers, labourer's, storehouses, and industrial buildings. Although some may have been strictly the centre of large farms, others included industry in the form of pottery and metalworking. Individual houses were as different then as they are now, but the villas followed some general patterns. They were half-timber frame houses on stone foundations, one story in height, capped with slate or clay tiled roofs. Under floor heating systems were universal. Tile floors were common, and most large villas contained at least one room with a mosaic floor. Walls may have been decorated with mosaics or painted scenes. Furniture was made of wood, in patterns similar to Roman style throughout the Empire. Many villas also had separate bath houses. The golden age of the Roman villa in Britain was in the 2nd and 3rd centuries. After that they fell into disuse or were taken over for other purposes…

Roman Britain

Life in a Roman market town.

Summary of Roman Britain

Trade in Roman Britain:

Industry in various forms was encouraged by the Romans. In their bid for the veneer of civilisation the elite of Britain imported Roman wine, jewellery, and pottery. In return they exported cattle, grain, lead, iron, tin, and, curiously enough, hunting dogs. The local pottery industries throughout Britain flourished, as did iron working. The large standing Roman army in Britain, as many as 40,000 troops for long periods of time, was a natural market energizer for British industry, and the extensive Roman road network helped speed the transport of goods throughout the island. Despite the growth of towns and bureaucracy and all the other essentials of civilisation that came with the Roman conquest, the lot of the majority of Britons was unchanged. Britain was an agricultural province, dependent on small farms. The lives of the farmers changed very little. They still built round Celtic huts and worked the same fields in the same way. Their standard of living changed little, if at all. Despite the veneer of Roman civilisation, Britain was still largely a Celtic, or even a Neolithic society…

Roman Britain

Roman army shields ready and waiting for action…

Summary of Roman Britain

The Boudica rebellion in Roman Britain 60 AD:

In 60 AD trouble flared up in East Anglia, while Roman troops were busy in the final battle with the Druids on Anglesey Island (Wales). To understand what happened, you have to go back to the idea of client Kingship. The Iceni tribe, lived in what is now modern Norfolk (where I live today), had reached an accommodation with the Romans, keeping their own territory in exchange for not making a fuss. It started when the Iceni king, Prasutagas, decided that it would be prudent to make his will assigning half of his personal property to the Roman emperor. When he died the Roman officials decided to interpret his will as a submission to the Roman state, so they moved to appropriate all of the Iceni lands and disarm the tribe. Prasutagas had a widow called Boudica (or Boadicea as she is sometimes known) protested. The Romans had her flogged and her daughters were raped. This high handed treatment of an ostensible ally had predictable results. Queen Boudica raised the Iceni and with the help of the neighbouring Trinivantes tribe she led a revolt against Roman rule. The capital at Colchester was burned, as was London and Verulamium, near modern St.Albans.

Norfolk's Queen Boudica…

Boudica's treatment of her enemies was fierce and she must have given the Romans a terrific scare. One legion was so terrified that they refused to move against her. She was eventually brought to bay at an unknown site by a much smaller force of Roman troops. The battle turned against her when the Celts became entangled with their own camp followers and were massacred. It is said that Boudica herself took poison rather than face capture. The upshot of the Boudica revolt was that the Iceni territory was ravaged and much of the province was put under military rule…

Roman Britain

A major Roman City

The Romans and the Iceni do battle

Roman Britain

The Roman baths in the City of Bath

Roman mosaic floor from a villa which would soon be abandoned as the Romans left and the Anglo Saxons arrived in Great Britain and that is who we are going to meet next …

Anglo-Saxon Britain

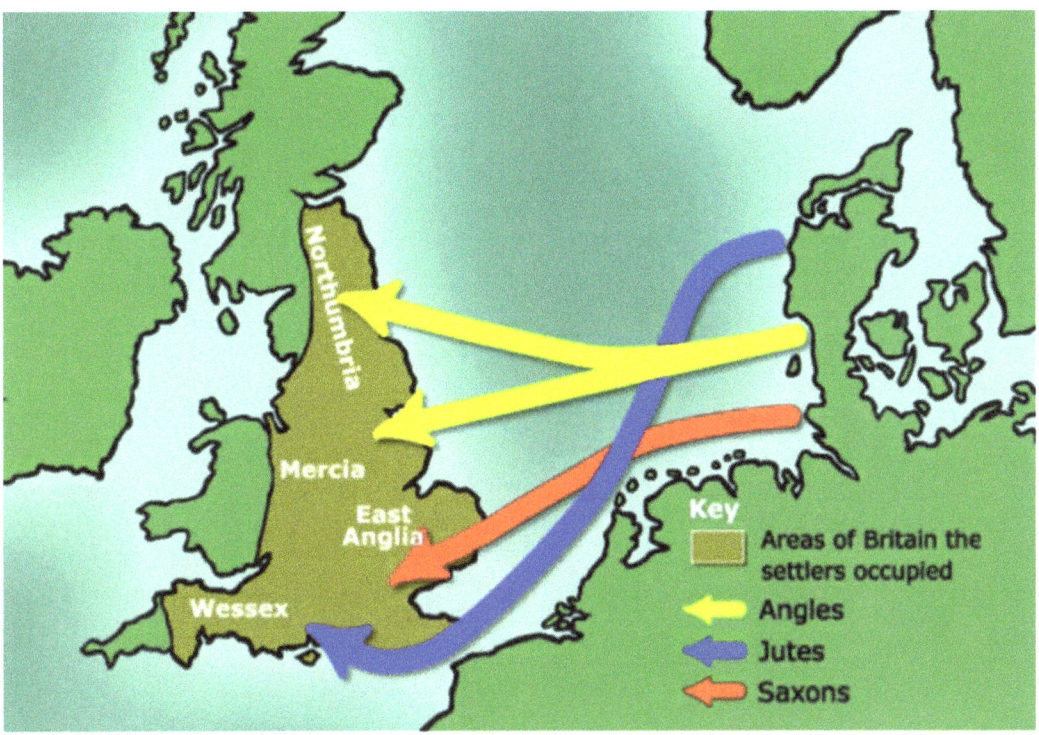

Map showing the flow of people into Britain

The very early medieval period saw a series of invasions of Britain by the Germanic Speaking Saxons, beginning in the 5th century. Anglo-Saxon Kingdoms were formed and gradually came to cover the territory of present-day England. Around 600 AD, seven principal Kingdoms had emerged, beginning the so-called period of the Heptarchy. Christianity was brought into England during this period and it soon spread to the rest of Great Britain…

Anglo-Saxon Britain

An Anglo-Saxon warrior

One of the best archeological discoveries of the last century was found at Sutton Hoo, near Woodbridge, in the English county of Suffolk. It is the site of two 6th- and early 7th-century cemeteries. One contained an undisturbed ship burial, including a wealth of Anglo-Saxon artefacts of outstanding archaeological significance, these are now held in the British Museum in London. Use of the site culminated at a time when Raedwald, the ruler of the East Angles, held senior power among the English people and played a dynamic if ambiguous part in the establishment of Christian ruler ship in England. It is generally thought most likely that he is the person buried in the ship. The site has been vital in the understanding of the Anglo-Saxon Kingdom of East Anglia and the whole early Anglo-Saxon period in Britain…

Anglo-Saxon Britain

Eric the Viking…

The Vikings are coming:

This cry brought terror to all the people of Great Britain and much has been said about these fearsome warriors. In the 9th century AD the Vikings from Denmark and Norway conquered most of England. Only the Kingdom of Wessex under Alfred the Great survived and even managed to re-conquer and unify England for much of the 10th century, before a new series of Danish raids in the late 10th century AD and early 11th century AD culminated in the wholesale subjugation of England to Denmark under Canute the Great. Danish rule was overthrown however, and the local House of Wessex was restored to power in Great Britain under Edward the Confessor for about two decades until his death in 1066. After the summary of the Anglo Saxon period and some Anglo-Saxon pictures we will march into the age of the Normans…

Anglo-Saxon Britain

An Anglo-Saxon King

Summary of Anglo-Saxon Britain

We know very little of the first few hundred years of the Anglo-Saxon era, or of the "English", era, primarily because the invaders were an illiterate people. Our earliest records of them are little more than highly inventive lists of rulers. We know that they established separate kingdoms, the Saxons settling in the south and west, the Angles in the east and north, and the Jutes on the Isle of Wight and the mainland opposite. They probably thought of themselves as separate peoples, but they shared a common language and similar customs. One of these customs was fighting everyone in sight. A King's power was not hereditary; it depended solely on his ability to win battles and so gain land, treasure, and slaves to give his supporters. He was obliged to fight and keep on fighting. If not, he would find himself out of a job or deprived of his life, or both…

Anglo-Saxon Britain

An Anglo-Saxon King and an Anglo Saxon house

Summary of Anglo-Saxon Britain

Succession from father to son was never a foregone conclusion. Any relative of the old King who could muster enough support could make a bid for the throne. This helps to explain why the Anglo-Saxon Kingdoms came and went so quickly. The power of any Kingdom over its neighbours was only as solid as the strength of its King in battle. The 7th century was the age of Northumbrian ascendance, with Mercia playing second fiddle. In the 8th century these roles reversed…

Anglo-Saxon Britain

The Anglo-Saxon Kings of Sutton Hoo

Summary of Anglo-Saxon Britain

The most powerful and well known of the Mercian Kings was Offa, who ruled from 758-796 AD. A successful warrior (which is a given for anyone in those days who managed to hold onto power for so long), he defeated the Kings of Sussex, Anglia, and Wessex, proclaiming himself King of the English. King Offa then caused to be built the earthwork that still bears his name, Offa's Dyke, which stretches the 150 mile length of the Welsh border. Begun in the 780's AD, the purpose of the dyke seems to have been as a fortified frontier barrier, much as Hadrian's Wall some six centuries previous. In most places the ditch was 25 feet from the bottom of the cut to the top of the bank, with wood or stone walling on top of that. The work involved has been compared to the building of the Great Pyramid in Egypt…

Anglo-Saxon Britain

Anglo-Saxon village

Summary of Anglo-Saxon Britain

The building of the dyke gives us some idea of the power wielded by Offa. It seems that the dyke was not permanently manned, the Mercians relying instead on the warning given by a series of beacons. The upper hand enjoyed by the Mercians did not long survive Offa's death. In the 820's AD a series of victories by Egbert, king of Wessex, broke Mercian control in the south east. The 9th century AD may well have turned into a struggle for the upper hand between Mercia and Wessex if not for one thing; England was once again the subject of recurring raids from across the seas. This time it was the Danes and Norwegians. The Danes attacked the east coast of England where I live today, the Norwegians attacked the north by way of Ireland and Scotland…

Anglo-Saxon Britain

Viking warrior and a Viking long ship.

Summary of Anglo-Saxon Britain

The Vikings are coming:

The Vikings were people from Denmark (The Danes). The Danes found rich pickings in the undefended monastic settlements on Lindisfarne Island and Jarrow in Northumbria, but they were not out solely out for loot. The Danish raids were partly a response to population pressures in their homeland, so they wanted new lands to settle, not merely easy plunder. They made good use of fortified settlements as bases to expand, and their use of helmets, shields, chain mail, and particularly the long handled battle axe, meant they were better armed than most of their foes…

Anglo-Saxon Britain

Sutton Hoo Kings death/war mask

Anglo-Saxon warriors

Anglo-Saxon Britain

Anglo-Saxon kitchen equipment

Anglo-Saxon coins

Anglo-Saxon Britain

Anglo-Saxon village life

An Anglo-Saxon hall

Anglo-Saxon Britain

What the well dressed Anglo-Saxon looked like

An Anglo-Saxon comb

Anglo-Saxon Britain

An Anglo-Saxon treasure

An Anglo-Saxon coin horde

Anglo-Saxon Britain

Peaceful Anglo-Saxon village before the Normans arrive

Anglo Saxons at war

Now as we march onward from the Anglo Saxon era we find ourselves facing a new invader called the Normans…

Norman Britain

In 1066, William the Conqueror, Duke of Normandy said said he was the rightful heir to the English throne, invaded England, and defeated King Harold at the Battle of Hastings.

Most children learn in school today about the arrow that is said to have hit King Harold in the eye but fail to grasp that this event heralded the introduction of the great buildings of the Normans. The Norman King led his troops personally into battle at Hastings and after this success he was indeed the "Conqueror" of Anglo Saxon Britain. He then divided his new Kingdom up amongst his Norman Knights and so started the rule of the Normans in Great Britain…

Norman Britain

The Normans invading Britain and a Norman castle in England

Proclaiming himself to be King William I, he strengthened his regime by appointing loyal members of the Norman elite to many positions of authority, building a system of castles across the country and ordering a census of his new kingdom, the Domesday Book. Copies of the Domesday Book still exist today and form an important source of research for historians and can be even viewed on line. The Late Medieval period was characterised by many battles between England and France, coming to a head in the Hundred Years' War from which France emerged victorious. The monarchs throughout the Late Medieval period belonged to the houses of Plantaganet, Lancaster and York. Our journey will now move into the era called Tudor Britain after a summary of Norman Britain and have a look at some more pictures of Norman Britain…

Norman Britain

Summary of Norman Britain

William the Conqueror was an innovator in government. He built a strong centralized administration staffed with his Norman supporters. He was also not about to put up with any backtalk from the newly conquered English. He subdued the south and east easily, but the north rose in rebellion. William's response was the ferocious "Harrying of the North" (1069-70 AD), which devastated the land in a broad swath from York to Durham. The results of this burning and destruction left much of the area depopulated for centuries. Following on the heels of northern resistance the most famous English rebel of them all, Hereward the Wake, stirred up resistance to the Norman conquerors in East Anglia from a base at Ely (just down the road from where I live), deep in the fenland (again another link to Norfolk my home county). Eventually Hereward, too, was subdued, perhaps bought off, and the land was William's to hold. One of the ways he insured that he held it was to build castles everywhere. These were often hurried affairs in a continental "motte and bailey" design, usually first in wood, only later replaced with stone. Most castles were built with forced local labour on land confiscated from English rebels…

Norman Britain

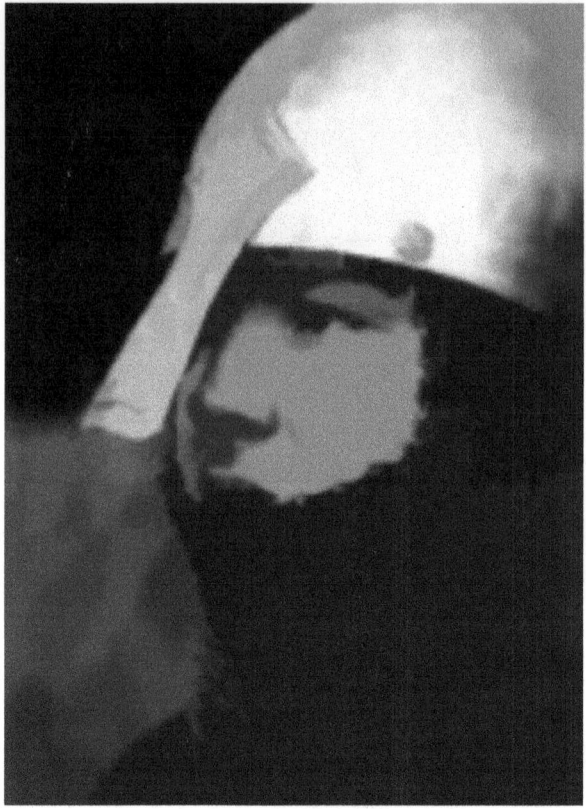

A Norman soldier

Summary of Norman Britain

The Domesday Book is probably the thing for which William I is best remembered, aside from winning the battle of Hastings and making England a European kingdom, is the Domesday Book. The Domesday Book was, in effect, the first national census. It was a royal survey of all England for administration and tax purposes. William needed proper records so that his new, efficient Norman bureaucracy could do its job, especially when it came to collecting all the revenues due to the crown. Inspectors were sent into every part of England to note the size, ownership, and resources of each hide of land. Contrary to popular belief, some small areas did seem to have escaped the assessors notice, but for the times the Domesday Book represented an amazing accomplishment. It has also left exact records behind which give the historians of today a lot of data about life in Norman England…

Norman Britain

Normans coming to Great Britain and a Norman Knight

Summary of Norman Britain

William the Conquer had many castles built by his Barons so they could hold the Kingdom for the King. In theory every inch of English land belonged to the crown and William's vassals had to swear fealty directly to the crown. Contrast this with the earlier Saxon practice where each man swore allegiance to the person of his lord. Now William was making loyalty to the nation, in the form of the crown, supersede loyalty to the individual person of a lord. Anglo-Saxon churchmen were replaced gradually by Normans appointed by William. Under the administration of Lanfranc, Norman Archbishop of Canterbury, new monasteries were founded, while rules and discipline were enforced more stringently. Church and lay justice were separated; the bishops were given their own courts, allowing common law to evolve independently. William retained the right to appoint bishops and impeach abbots. He used these churchmen as his major administrators, which made perfect sense, for they were by far the best educated members of society. Indeed, they were often the only educated members of society…

Norman Britain

A Norman farm

Coins of the Norman period

Selby abbey

Norman Britain

Norman soldiers

Norman Britain

A Norman castle

The Norman castle in Norwich

Norman Britain

The Norman Cathedral in Norwich

The Normans built many great buildings in Great Britain many of which still stands today. One of these is the cathedral in Norwich. This is the City where I was born and raised before moving into the North Norfolk countryside. But, over time, the Normans gradually faded away and were replaced by the Tudor Kings and that is who we are going to meet next!...

Tudor Britain

The Tudor period is the period from 1485 to 1603 AD. In England and Wales it coincides with the rule of the Tudor dynasty in England. The first Tudor monarch was Henry VII (1457–1509). England was economically healthier, more expansive, and more optimistic under the Tudors than at any time in the previous thousand years. The term Tudor was seldom used in the 16th century, because the Kings and Queens did not like being reminded of their origins in the humble Tudor family.

Henry VII began the move towards royal absolutism. This was a belief in the divine right of Kings to rule as they saw fit, without having to answer to nobles, church, or Parliament. Whatever else he was, Henry was an able and active administrator. He was frugal to the point of parsimony. When he came to the throne, the crown was heavily in debt, but when he died he left his son Henry a bulging treasury. What his son did with that money is another story. Henry's reign saw the beginning of the Court of Star Chamber, so called because the room where they met was decorated with paintings of stars. This court was closed, and was answerable to no one but the king. It eventually became synonymous with secretive and autocratic administration. After a summary and pictures of Tudor Britain this dynasty disappears and Britain becomes the realm of the Stuart Kings and Queens…

Tudor Britain

Summary of Tudor Britain

Rebellions in Tudor Britain:

Henry had to deal with two rebellions during his reign, both by probable imposters claiming to be legitimate heirs to the throne. First there was Lambert Simnel, who was eventually captured and made to work as a scullery in Henry's kitchens. He was followed by Perkin Warbeck, who gathered foreign support for an invasion. Warbeck was defeated and eventually hanged with some of his supporters. Henry VII's eldest son was Arthur, Prince of Wales. He married Catherine of Aragon, but died shortly thereafter, leaving the throne to fall to his younger brother Henry. History has not proved kind to the memory of Henry VIII. He is often remembered as the grossly stout, overbearing tyrant of his later years. In his youth, however, Henry was everything it was thought a king should be. A natural athlete, a gifted musician and composer, Henry was erudite, religious, and a true leader among the monarchs of his day. An older but no wiser Henry VIII. Henry had none of his father's drive for the grind of administration. He handed over that role to his advisor, Cardinal Thomas Wolsey. Henry was more concerned with cutting a fine figure than with balancing rows of figures like his father, and the result was predictable. Over the course of his reign he managed to turn a bulging treasury into a gaping black-hole of debt. Thomas Wolsey was the son of a Suffolk wool merchant. He became in turn Bishop of London, Archbishop of York, Cardinal and Lord Chancellor, and papal legate. He was even at one time considered seriously as a candidate for the papacy itself. Wolsey loved luxury and ostentation. He maintained a household of over 1000 people, and at the height of his power he was more of a King than poor old Henry himself…

Tudor Britain

Tudor dress

Summary of Tudor Britain

Religious reformers in Tudor Britain:

The whole of Europe was ablaze during Henry VIII's time with the religious need for Reformation. Great reformers, religious and secular, called England home. Erasmus, scholar and monk, taught at Oxford, where he agitated for reform within the church. Sir Thomas More, later Chancellor, wrote Utopia, a vision of an ideal society with no church at all to get in the way of spiritual understanding. Henry himself, despite his later break with Rome, was not a religious reformer. He was fairly orthodox in his own beliefs, and he passed measures against Lutheranism and upheld many traditional Catholic rites from attack by reformers. Upon marriage to Catherine, Henry received a special dispensation from the pope in order to marry his brother's widow, Catherine. The only child of that marriage was a daughter, Mary. Henry desperately wanted a male heir, and as time went on it became obvious that Catherine would have no more children. Henry began to cast around for a solution. Henry decided that he had, had enough of his marriage, and started eyeing one of the Queen's ladies in waiting, Anne Boleyn. Anne refused Henry's advances without the benefit of a wedding, so Henry sent his chancellor, Cardinal Wolsey, to ask the pope for an annulment of his marriage to Catherine. Unfortunately for the powerful Wolsey, he failed, and was deposed from office. Even the "gift" of his magnificent new palace at Hampton Court to Henry could not save Wolsey, who died shortly after his deposition, saving Henry the bother of a mock trial for treason…

Tudor Britain

A splendid Tudor stain glass window

Summary of Tudor Britain

Thomas More:

In Wolsey's place Thomas More was brought in to be Chancellor. Henry's situation was now desperate, for Anne was pregnant, and at all costs the child, which Henry was sure must be a son, had to be legitimate. Henry got Parliament to declare that his first marriage was void, and he secretly married Anne. It was Unfortunately for Henry, the child proved to be female once again, the future Elizabeth I. Over the next several years Henry's wrangle with the pope grew ever deeper, until in 1534 AD the Act of Supremacy was passed, making Henry, not the pope but the head of the church in England. This was not at first a doctrinal split in any way, but a personal and political move. Henry VIII was able to split from Rome because, for one thing, the church had incurred a tremendous amount of bad feeling over the years. High church officials were seen as rich, indolent, and removed from the people they were supposed to be serving. The abbeys and monasteries were well off, and certainly subject to jealousy. Feelings against priests and churchmen in general ran high. The church had become too far removed from its spiritual roots and purpose. Starting small Henry VIII took the most decisive step against the power of the church in 1538 AD, when he began the Dissolution of the Monasteries. He did it piecemeal, perhaps to avoid too much outcry at the start. First the small, less powerful houses had their property confiscated and their buildings blighted (made unsuitable for use). They were then followed the next year by the large houses…

Tudor Britain

A Tudor house…

Summary of Tudor Britain

The Dissolution of the Monasteries in Tudor Britain:

Philosophical concepts of the power of the king over church may have played a part in Henry's decision to suppress the monasteries, but so did greed. The monasteries were rich, and a lot of that wealth found its way directly or indirectly to the royal treasury. Some of the monastery buildings were sold to wealthy gentry for use as country estates. Many others became sources of cheap building materials for local inhabitants. One of the results of the Dissolution of the Monasteries is that those who bought the old monastic lands were inclined to support Henry in his break with Rome, purely from self-interest. Henry VIII wanted money, Parliament wanted to raise money without having to impose unpopular taxes, the gentry saw a chance to increase their own estates, and the merchant middle class saw a chance to become landed gentry themselves. Henry sold the monastic lands for bargain basement prices, such was his need for ready cash. The real beneficiary of the Dissolution was not the king, but the new class of gentry who bought the lands. The suppression of the monasteries and places of pilgrimages was devastating for those pilgrimage centres that had no other economic base. Income from the people on the pilgrim routes dropped, with no way to recover it. The other great loser of the Dissolution was culture; many monastic libraries full of priceless illuminated manuscripts were destroyed, with little or no regard for their value. The monks and nuns were treated quite well as a rule. Only a few who resisted were summarily executed. The English Reformation was slow to gather steam. Catholics were not mistreated (at least not at first), and in many parts of the country religious life went on unchanged. Catholic rites and symbols remained in use for many years…

Tudor Britain

Soldiers ruthlessly putting down the Kett revolt

Summary of Tudor Britain

Robert Kett:

Robert Kett was a yeoman farmer, a native of Wymondham, Norfolk. Yet again we find a Norfolk person making history. It makes me very proud to be a Norfolk boy and to hear about all the significant things, throughout history, people from my county have been involved in. We know little of Robert Kett's early life, but we certainly know about the end of it. In 1549 Kett led a rebellion against the practice of enclosure of common land, but the story is more complex than that. In order to understand the rebellion and the light in which authorities saw it, you have to look at two events that created enormous social turmoil in early 16th century AD England; the enclosure movement and the dawn of the Reformation. One of the traditional rights enjoyed by Kett and his social equals was the right to graze animals on common land. However, in the Tudor period local land owners (the nobility and rising merchant classes) began to enclose common land and use it to graze their own sheep, in the process removing that formerly accessible land from farming by villagers and small holding farmers. This enclosure allowed landowners to create great wealth by selling wool. English wool was the life-blood of the economy in many areas of the country throughout the late medieval and Tudor periods. By enclosing common land and using it to raise sheep, landowners became rich, but at the same time, peasants and yeoman farmers like Kett, who used common land for subsistence farming and raising animals, now found it hard to survive, let alone thrive…

Tudor Britain

Tudors marching to the sound of the drums

Summary of Tudor Britain

Kett's Rebellion:

Out of these twin streams of unrest came the violent events of 1549 that culminated in Kett's Rebellion. In a sense the alliance of religion and land reform protest was unfortunate, because when religion was linked to very real social concerns over land enclosure, the authorities lumped both together and saw all the unrest as a Catholic rising. And by the reasoning of the time, a rebellion over religion was a rebellion directly against the crown; it was treason, and had to be treated as such. Robert Kett (or Ket as it sometimes spelled) was what we would today call upper middle-class. He made a great deal of money in business, and owned a sizeable amount of land. He possessed several manors, and had even engaged in a couple of land deals with the Earl of Warwick, which would prove rather ironic as events turned out. Like many of his fellow landowners, Kett decided to put up fences, to enclose local common land to his own benefit. What he did not know was how his actions would affect the livelihood of poor farmers and peasants who depended upon using common land to farm and to graze their animals. In the summer of 1549 AD the local peasants rebelled, and began to tear down the fences. When they came to Kett's land, instead of reacting with violence himself, Kett listened to their tale of hardship. The more he listened, the more convinced he became of the truth of their grievances. Kett himself helped tear down the fences he had just recently erected. Later he became the leader of the rebel cause…

Tudor Britain

Time for a meal in the troubled Tudor times

Summary of Tudor Britain

Kett's Rebellion:

Under Kett the rebels marched from Wymondham to Norwich, the City of my birth, and as they marched, their numbers swelled. By the time they reached Norwich they numbered several thousand. The city government, faced with thousands of rebellious peasants, not surprisingly refused to let them enter, so Kett set up a camp on Mousehold Heath. From there he tried to negotiate with Norwich's leaders. After a certain amount of talk, an order arrived from the king (in fact, from the king's council, for Edward VI was still a minor), and the city firmly told Kett that his band would not be allowed to enter the city. Kett then attempted to cross Bishop Bridge, but the bridge was held by a small garrison. The rebels fired at the bridge and the nearby Cow Tower. They did some damage to the top of the tower, and must have softened up the defenders on the bridge, for when they attacked the bridge a second time they drove the defenders back and were able to cross the River Wensum and gain the city. Once inside the city there was certainly some violence. The rebels seized the Mayor, Thomas Codd, and killed several officials. But Kett was not interested in mob violence or plundering Norwich; he was interested in righting a social wrong and with creating a more just society. Under Kett the rebels set up a new form of local government, and a court to hear cases brought by commoners. Many of the court cases were held in the open air, under a '*tree of reformation*'. Predictably perhaps, many of the accused brought before the rebel court were local gentry, accused of wrongs against the working classes. Most were found guilty and imprisoned or some may have even been hanged!…

Tudor Britain

Tudor people in their homes

Summary of Tudor Britain

Kett's Rebellion:

News of Kett's rebellion spread throughout East Anglia, and sympathetic revolts broke out across the entire region. The government sent an army to deal with the rebels, under the leadership of the Marquis of Northampton. The Royal army, perhaps surprisingly, was soundly beaten by the rebels under Kett's command. Kett held Norwich and a large swath of the countryside surrounding the city. The government had to act before the rebellion took an even greater hold. They sent a new, much larger army, under the Earl of Warwick. Warwick's army defeated the rebels after a bloody fight, and forced them out of the city, back to Mousehold Heath. But Warwick lacked the manpower to take on the rebel force in an open battle. He found himself trapped inside Norwich, a prisoner inside the city walls. Reminders of these bloody days are everywhere in Norwich. The Earl had his cavalry stable their horses in The Halls, formerly a Dominican friary. He himself made his headquarters in the house of Augustine Steward, a wealthy merchant. A game of cat and mouse ensued. Each night the rebels would sneak into the city, seize food and supplies, and waylay government soldiers. Soon, however, reinforcements arrived, and Warwick had enough manpower to counter-attack, and to defend the city from rebel incursions. Now the rebels were deprived of their supplies, and the tide turned. Kett knew he could not maintain the fight without access to the food stored in Norwich. He decided to gamble everything on one big battle. On 27 August 1549 AD Kett's rebels met Warwick's government army at Dussindale, a small valley outside the city. The rebels outnumbered Warwick's army, but they had no cavalry, and that was what sealed their fate. The royal forces were utterly triumphant, killing thousands of rebels and taking thousands more captive…

Tudor Britain

Bringing in the harvest during the Tudor period

Summary of Tudor Britain

Kett's Rebellion:

Robert Kett was captured a few miles from the battle site. He was taken to the Tower of London, held for a time, he was then tried for treason. The outcome of the trial was a foregone conclusion. He was found guilty, and transported back to Norwich to be executed. He was hanged in chains from the walls of Norwich Castle, and allowed to die of starvation. His corpse was left hanging long after his death, to act as a warning to the people of Norwich of the fate that awaited traitors. It bothered the authorities that 'one of their own' had led the rebellion. Over the years official accounts tried to cast Kett as a peasant, a tanner, a member of the working classes. He was not. He was a member of the minor gentry, a man of high principle, who came to believe that justice should apply equally to all, regardless of social standing or wealth. Over the years Robert Kett became a symbol of the struggle for basic human rights. In 1949 AD, on the 400th anniversary of his rebellion, the city of Norwich put up a plaque on the wall of Norwich Castle, near the main entrance. The plaque reads: In 1549 AD Robert Kett, yeoman farmer of Wymondham, was executed by hanging in this castle after the defeat of the Norfolk rebellion of which he was the leader. In 1949 AD, four hundred years later, this memorial was placed here by the citizens of Norwich in reparation and honour to a notable and courageous leader in the long struggle of the common people of England to escape from a servile life into the freedom of just conditions…

Tudor Britain

King Henry VIII

Queen Elizabeth I

Tudor Britain

The dining room of a Tudor house

The Tudors at home

Tudor Britain

The Tudor dance

Bread and wine for after the dance but we will leave it alone and dance our way into Stuart Britain…

Stuart Britain

The Stuart period is the period from 1603 AD to 1714 AD and from 1371 AD in Scotland. The House of Stuarts first monarch was James VI of Scotland. The period ended with the death of Queen Anne and the accession of George I from the House of Hanover. The Stuart period was plagued by internal and religious strife, and a large-scale civil war. There was a short-lived republic, the first time that the country had experienced such an event. The Restoration of the Crown was soon followed by another 'Glorious' Revolution. William and Mary of Orange ascended the throne as joint monarchs and defenders of Protestantism, followed by Queen Anne, the second of James II's daughters. The end of the Stuart line with the death of Queen Anne led to the drawing up of the Act of Settlement in 1701, which provided that only Protestants could hold the throne…

Stuart Britain

Summary of Stuart Britain

The Tudor Queen Elizabeth I was followed to the throne by James VI of Scotland, who became James I of England. James believed in the absolute power of the monarchy, and he had a rocky relationship with an increasingly vociferous and demanding Parliament. It would be a mistake to think of Parliament as a democratic institution, or the voice of the common citizen. Parliament was a forum for the interests of the nobility and the merchant classes (not unlike today, some would say). James VI was a firm protestant, and in 1604 AD he expelled all Catholic priests from the island. This was one of the factors which led to the Gunpowder Plot of 1605 AD. A group of Catholic plotters planned to blow up Parliament when it opened on November 5th. However, an anonymous letter betrayed the plot and one of the plotters, Guy Fawkes, was captured in the cellars of the Houses of Parliament with enough gunpowder to blow the place sky high. Most of the plotters were captured and executed (this event is still celebrated today on "Fireworks Night" on the 5th November each year). It was during James VI reign that radical Protestant groups called Puritans began to gain a sizeable following. Puritans wanted to "purify" the church by paring down church ritual, educating the clergy, and limiting the powers of bishops. King James resisted this last aim. The powers of the church and King were too closely linked. "No Bishop, No King," he said. The Puritans also favoured thrift, education, and individual initiative, therefore they found great support among the new middle class of merchants who held the most power in the Commons. James' attitude toward Parliament was clear. He commented in 1614 AD that he was surprised his ancestors should have permitted such an institution to come into existence. It is sedition in subjects to dispute what a King may do in the height of his power. In 1611 AD the King James Version of the Holy Bible was issued, the result of seven years of labour by the best translators and theological minds of the day. It remained the authoritative, though not necessarily the most accurate, version of the Bible for centuries…

Stuart Britain

Stuart King Charles I…

Summary of Stuart Britain

Charles I (1625-49 AD) continued his father's acrimonious relationship with Parliament, squabbling over the right to levy taxes. Parliament responded with the Petition of Right in 1628 AD. It was the most dramatic assertion of the traditional rights of the English people since the Magna Carta. Its basic premise was that no taxes of any kind could be allowed without the permission of Parliament. Charles finally had enough, and in 1629 AD he dissolved Parliament and ruled without it for eleven years. Some of the ways he raised money during this period were of dubious legality by the standards of the time. Between 1630-43 AD large numbers of people emigrated from England as Archbishop Laud tried to impose uniformity on the church. Up to 60,000 people left, 1/3 of them to the new American colonies. Several areas lost a large part of their populations, and laws were enacted to curb the outflow. In 1634 AD Charles attempted to levy "ship-money", a tax that previously applied only to ports, on the whole country. This raised tremendous animosity throughout the realm. Finally Charles, desperate for money, summoned the so-called Short Parliament in 1640 AD. Parliament refused to vote Charles more money until its grievances were answered, and the king dismissed it after only three weeks. Then a rebellion broke out in Scotland and Charles was forced to call a new Parliament, dubbed the Long Parliament, which officially sat until 1660 AD. Parliament made increasing demands, which the king refused to meet. Neither side was willing to budge. Finally in 1642 AD fighting broke out. The English Civil War (1642-1646 AD) polarized society largely along class lines. Parliament drew most of its support from the middle classes, while the king was supported by the nobility, the clergy, and the peasantry. Parliamentary troops were known as Roundheads because of their severe hair style. The king's army were known as Cavaliers, from the French for "knight", or "horseman"…

Stuart Britain

The English Civil War…

Summary of Stuart Britain

The war began as a series of indecisive skirmishes notable for not much beyond the emergence of a Parliamentary general from East Anglia named Oliver Cromwell. Cromwell whipped his irregular volunteer troops into the disciplined New Model Army. Meanwhile, Charles established the royalist headquarters in Oxford, called his own Parliament, and issued his own money. To the poor, the turmoil over religion around the Civil War meant little. They were bound by tradition and they supported the king, as they always had. Charles encouraged poor relief, unemployment measures, price controls, and protection for small farmers. For most people, life during the Civil War went on as before. Few were involved or even knew about the fighting. In 1644 AD a farmer at Marston Moor was told to clear out because the armies of Parliament and the king were preparing to fight. "What?" he exclaimed, "Has them two fallen out, then?" The turning point of the war was probably that same Battle of Marston Moor in 1644 AD. Charles' troops under his nephew Prince Rupert were soundly beaten by Cromwell, giving Parliament control of the north of England. Above the border Lord Montrose captured much of Scotland for Charles, but was beaten at Philiphaugh and Scot support was lost for good. The Parliamentary cause became increasingly entangled with extreme radical Protestantism. In 1645 AD Archbishop Laud was executed, and in the same year the Battle of Naseby spelled the end of the royalist hopes. Hostilities dragged on for another year, and the Battle of Stow-on-the-Wold (1646) was the last armed conflict of the war. Charles rather foolishly stuck to his absolutist beliefs and refused every proposal made by Parliament and the army for reform. He preferred to try to play them against each other through intrigue and deception. He signed a secret treaty which got the Scots to rise in revolt, but that threat was snuffed out at Preston pans (1648 AD). Finally, the radical core of Parliament had enough. They believed that only the execution of the king could prevent the kingdom from descending into anarchy. Charles was tried for treason in 1649 AD, before a Parliament whose authority he refused to acknowledge. He was executed outside Inigo Jones' Banqueting Hall at Whitehall on January 30th…

Stuart Britain

Summary of Stuart Britain

Oliver Cromwell: Oliver Cromwell was born on April 25, 1599 AD, in Huntingdon, near Cambridge. His father Robert was the younger son of a knight, which in those days meant that he had very little property. Cromwell grew up in genteel poverty; not quite a member of the nobility, yet not a commoner either. In 1620 he married Elizabeth Bourchier. For the early part of his adult life, Oliver scraped along, barely making ends meet on the scraps he had inherited from his father. Then in 1630 AD the failure of his business caused him to move to St. Ives and begin again as a yeoman farmer. However in 1637 he inherited a modest income and property when his mother's brother died without heir. Despite Cromwell's impoverished circumstances, he had many opportunities to interact with powerful figures at court. His grandfather lived in state at his house outside Huntingdon, where he frequently entertained royalty and court officials. And through his wife's father, Sir James Bourchier, Cromwell was brought into contact with London merchants and leading Puritan figures. In 1630 AD Cromwell suffered what we would today term a mental breakdown. At the same time he underwent a powerful religious conversion to the Puritan cause. He afterwards said that he felt as though he was waiting for God to give him a mission. In the meantime Cromwell was elected as a Member of Parliament for Huntingdon, a post he owed more to patronage and aristocratic connections than to any great merit. He attended the Parliament of 1628-9 AD (and was likely the poorest MP there). He seems to have been overawed by his elevated status, and hardly made any contribution to the Parliamentary sessions. However, in 1640 AD Cromwell was back in Parliament, this time representing Cambridge. And this time he had quite a lot to say! He was one of the most outspoken critics of royal policies and of the established Anglican Church. He also advocated increased Parliamentary powers, calling for annual sessions of Parliament, and for Parliament, not the King, to have the power to name army generals…

Stuart Britain

Summary of Stuart Britain

Oliver Cromwell: When fighting finally broke out in 1642 AD, Cromwell was named a captain of horse (a minor cavalry commander). But now his military leadership qualities came to the fore. Within a year he was Lieutenant General of Horse for the Army of the Eastern Association (essential equivalent to modern East Anglia). In 1645 AD, the three largest Parliamentary armies were combined. Parliamentary leaders could not agree on who should lead the cavalry of the new army, so they appointed Cromwell as temporary commander for 40 days. The temporary appointment was renewed many times over until finally becoming permanent in 1647 AD. His horsemen were responsible for major contributions to the victories at Marston Moor in 1644 AD and Naseby in 1645 AD. Cromwell wanted to settle for nothing less than total victory over the Cavaliers. Though he felt betrayed by Charles, Cromwell held out against a trial, and when he agreed it was with the idea that Charles would abdicate in favour of one of his sons. But Charles was obstinate to the last, and refused to step aside. After the death of Charles, further rebellions in favour of the future Charles II arose in Ireland and Scotland. Cromwell dealt with Ireland first, and his ferocious retribution for Irish actions earned him a reputation for cruelty. Scotland was next, and finally Cromwell defeated the younger Charles at the Battle of Worcester in 1651 AD. Cromwell then participated in the debates of the "Rump Parliament", which sat until 1653 AD. Finally, tired of the continuous bickering and lack of real desire for reform, he dissolved the Rump by the crude expediency of armed force. Finally, and probably with a sense of exasperation, Cromwell himself took up the reigns as Lord Protector, head of an executive council. Several efforts were made to have him named King, but this Cromwell resisted firmly. On September 3rd, 1658 AD, Oliver Cromwell died and was buried at Westminster Abbey. Charles II was called back from exile to resume the monarchy. In 1661 AD Oliver Cromwell's body was exhumed from its grave and hung at Tyburn. Then his head was cut off and put on public display for nearly 20 years outside Westminster Hall. The Stuart period eventually made way for the Georgian era…

Georgian Britain

A Georgian courtroom

The Georgian era is the period from 1714 AD to 1830 AD. This period of British History takes its name from, and is normally defined as spanning the reigns of, the first four Hanoverian Kings, of Great Britain who were all named George I, George II, George III and George IV. The era covers the period from 1714 AD to 1830 AD, with the sub-period of The Regency defined by the Regency of George IV as the Prince of Wales during the serious illness of his father King George III…

Georgian Britain

A Norfolk and Great British Hero - Horatio Nelson:

Nelson was born on 29 September 1758 AD in Burnham Thorpe, Norfolk. I would often cycle to Nelsons birthplace when I was a teenager to visit the rectory where he was born. Horatio Nelson was the sixth of the 11 children of a clergyman. He joined the navy aged 12, on a ship commanded by a maternal uncle. He became a captain at 20, and saw service in the West Indies, Baltic and Canada. He married Frances Nisbet in 1787 AD in Nevis, and returned to England with his bride to spend the next five years on half-pay, frustrated at the lack of a command. When Britain entered the French Revolutionary Wars in 1793 AD, Nelson was given command of the Agamemnon. In the battle at Calvi which is where he lost the sight in his right eye…

Georgian Britain

Lord Nelson at the Battle of the Nile in 1798 AD, successfully destroyed Napoleon's fleet and thus his bid for a direct trade route to India. Nelson's next posting took him to Naples, where he fell in love with Emma, Lady Hamilton. Although they remained in their respective marriages, Nelson and Emma Hamilton considered each other soul-mates and had a child together, called Horatia, in 1801 AD which was the same year Nelson was promoted to vice-admiral…

Georgian Britain

The Norfolk hero Horatio Nelson over the period 1794 AD to 1805 AD, under Nelson's leadership, the Royal Navy proved its supremacy over the French. His most famous engagement, at Cape Trafalgar, saved Britain from threat of invasion by Napoleon, but it would be his last. Before the battle on 21 October 1805 AD. Nelson sent out the famous signal to his fleet **' England expects that every man will do his duty'.** He was killed by a French sniper a few hours later while leading the attack on the combined French and Spanish fleet. His body was preserved in brandy and transported back to England where he was given a state funeral. His flag ship H.M.S Victory was sailed back to the UK and put as a permanent memorial to Nelson in a dry dock in Portsmouth where it can still be visited today…

Georgian Britain

Queen Victorian...

The last Hanoverian monarch of the UK was William's niece Queen Victoria, who is the namesake of the next historical era, the Victorian period, which is usually defined as occurring from the start of her reign, when William died, and continuing until her death. Before we venture on we will have a summary and some pictures of the Georgian times then we will be heading into the times of the British Empire which was at it's height in the Victorian period...

Georgian Britain

A Georgian artist at work

Summary of Georgian Britain

Georgian Britain commenced when Stuart Britain ceased when Queen Anne died without any heirs, the English throne was offered to her nearest Protestant relative, George of Hanover, who thus became George I of England. Throughout the long reign of George I, his son, and grandson, all named George, the very nature of English society and the political face of the realm changed. In part this was because the first two Georges took little interest in the politics of rule, and were quite content to let ministers rule on their behalf. These ministers, representatives of the king, or Prime Ministers, rather enjoyed ruling, and throughout this "Georgian period" the foundations of English political party system was solidified into something resembling what we have today. But more than politics changed; English society underwent a revolution in art and architecture. This was the age of the grand country house, when many of the great stately homes that we can visit today were built. Abroad, the English acquired more and more territory overseas through conquest and settlement, lands that would eventually make up The British Empire that stretched to every corner of the globe…

Georgian Britain

A fine Georgian house

A Georgian music night

Georgian Britain

An evening in a Georgian parlour

An evening in a Georgian public house

Georgian Britain

Georgian study with a globe of the world as a centre piece

Stevenson's Rocket

Georgian Britain

The inside of a Georgian house

The Georgian City of Bath

Georgian Britain

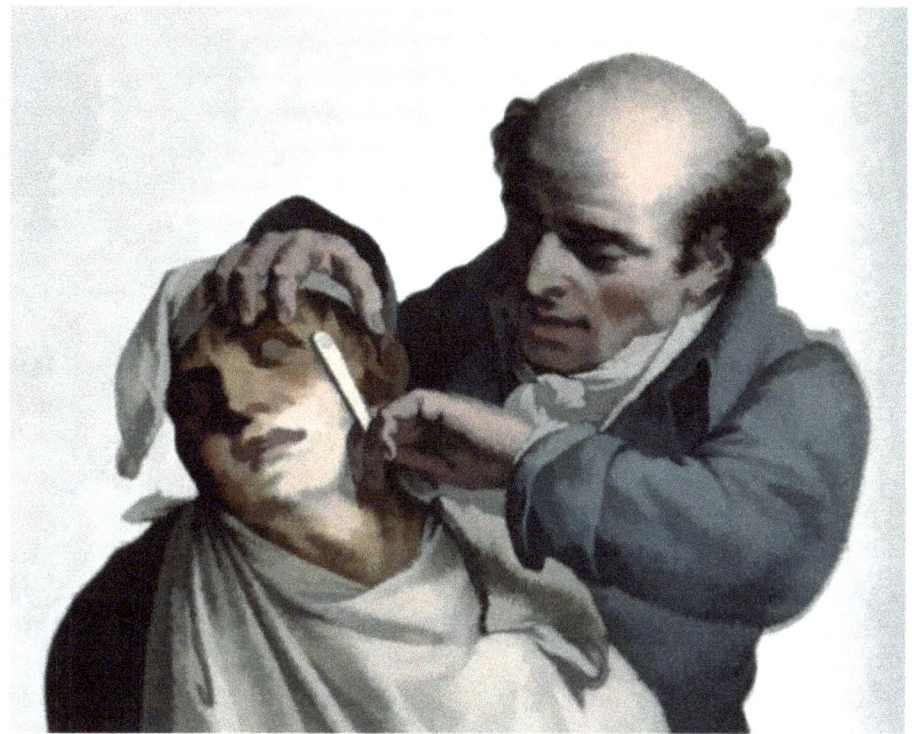

The Georgian barber

Barbers, at this time, also undertook blood letting and other minor treatments that were intended to cure aliments and conditions, that we would not dream of allowing our local hairdresser to perform today. Peoples appearance was very important to the well off Georgians and the rich spent fortunes on fancy cloths and hair styles. This was also the time of big grand houses and estates. It was however, not a very happy or contented time for the ordinary poor peasant…

Georgian Britain

A Georgian front door

A Georgian sitting room

Georgian Britain

In a Georgian music room

Georgian coinage

Victorian Britain

The Victorian era is the period of Great British history from 1837 to 1901. The Victorian era of British history (this also includes that of the British Empire) was the period of Queen Victoria's reign from 20 June 1837 AD until her death, on 22 January 1901 AD. It was a long period of peace, prosperity, refined sensibilities and national self-confidence for Great Britain…

Victorian Britain

Queen Victoria

The Victorians are renowned for their attitudes and culture that had a focus on the highly moralistic, straitlaced language and behaviour of their idea of what they saw as Victorian morality…

Victorian Britain

The Victorian era followed the Georgian period and preceded the Edwardian period. Culturally there was a transition away from the rationalism of the Georgian period and toward romanticism and mysticism with regard to religion, social values, and the arts…

Victorian Britain

In international relations the era was a long period of peace, colonial, and industrial consolidation, temporarily disrupted by the Crimean War in 1854. The end of the period saw the Boer War. Domestically, the agenda was increasingly liberal with a number of shifts in the direction of gradual political reform, industrial reform and the widening of the voting franchise…

Victorian Britain

During the early part of the Victorian era, the House of Commons was headed by two parties called the Whigs and the Conservatives. Two especially important figures in this period of British history are the prime ministers Gladstone and Disraeli, whose contrasting views changed the course of history. Disraeli, favoured by the queen, was a gregarious Tory. His rival Gladstone, a Liberal distrusted by the Queen, served more terms and oversaw much of the overall legislative development of the era…

Victorian Britain

The population of England and Wales almost doubled from 16.8 million in 1851 to 30.5 million in 1901. Scotland's population also rose rapidly, from 2.8 million in 1851 to 4.4 million in 1901. Ireland's population however decreased sharply, from 8.2 million in 1841 to less than 4.5 million in 1901, mostly due to the Great Famine. Around 15 million emigrants left the United Kingdom in the Victorian era, settling mostly in the United States, Canada, New Zealand and Australia...

Victorian Britain

Queen Victoria

Summary of Victorian Britain

The generally uneventful reign of George's brother, William IV (1830-37 AD), was followed by that of Queen Victoria (1837-1901 AD). Only 18 when she came to the throne, Victoria oversaw England at the height of its overseas power. The British Empire was established in her reign, and it reached its greatest expanse under her. Things did not start off smoothly, however. The Chartist movement began in 1839 AD with demands for electoral reform and universal male suffrage. The movement was taken over by radical reformers and was dealt with very harshly by the authorities. The Anti Corn Law League was another voice for social reform. They advocated total free trade, but it was not until 1846 AD that the Corn Laws were completely repealed…

Victorian Britain

A Victorian family

Summary of Victorian Britain

Victoria's consort, Prince Albert, was the main backer of the 1851 AD Great Exhibition. This was the first "world's fair", with exhibits from most of the world's nations. The exhibition was held in Hyde Park, and the showpiece was the Crystal Palace, a prefabricated steel and glass structure like a gigantic greenhouse, which housed the exhibits. The Crystal Palace was disassembled after the Exhibition and moved to Sydenham, in south London, where it burned down in 1936 AD. Overseas, England became involved in the Crimean War (1854 AD), which was notable only in that it provided evidence of military incompetence and the material for the poem "The Charge of the Light Brigade", by Alfred Tennyson. One positive that came out of the war was the establishment of more humane nursing practices under the influence of Florence Nightingale, the courageous "Lady with the Lamp"…

Victorian Britain

The Victorian industrial revolution in full swing

Summary of Victorian Britain

In 1857 AD Britain saw the Indian Mutiny. India had been administered by the East India Company with government co-operation. The spark for the Mutiny was provided when the army introduced new rifle cartridges which were rumoured to have been greased with lard. Any Hindu who bit off the end of the cartridge, which was essential practice when loading a gun, was committing sacrilege. The army rebelled and massacred many British officers, administrators, and families. After the Mutiny was put down the administration of India was taken over by the government of Britain. In Victorian times politics could have been called a tale of Two Prime Ministers. This era could be subtitled 'The Gladstone and Disraeli Show' for the two politicians who dominated it. The two men, Gladstone and Disraeli, could not have been more dissimilar. Gladstone was liberal, humanitarian, and devout. Queen Victoria found him stuffy. Disraeli, on the other hand, was imperialist, nationalistic, and charming to boot. The queen enjoyed his company, for he could make her laugh. This was also the age of the 'Irish Question', the question being whether or not the Irish should be allowed to rule themselves. Gladstone was a constant activist for increased Irish autonomy, but his views were not widely supported, and Irish extremists began a campaign of terrorism…

Victorian Britain

The narrow streets of a Victorian City

Summary of Victorian Britain

In Victorian Britain legal reform proceeded slowly. Education was made more accessible for the lower classes, and the Ballot Act of 1872 AD made voting a private affair for the first time. The Army Regulation Bill abolished the practice of purchasing commissions in the armed forces. Victorian literature. In this age before TV's, computers, and Nintendo, the most common form of entertainment was reading aloud (parents of the video age take note!). Writers like Dickens, Tennyson, and Trollop were widely read and discussed. The advent of universal compulsory education after 1870 AD meant that there was now a much larger audience for literature. Disraeli himself, when he wasn't locking horns with Gladstone, was a very popular novelist…

Victorian Britain

Children working in a Victorian mill

Summary of Victorian Britain

It was the time of the Victorian British Empire and much of the attention of the country was focused abroad during this era. In 1876 AD Victoria was declared Empress of India and the English Empire was constantly being expanded. The prevailing attitude in Britain was that expansion of British control around the globe was good for everyone. On the home front the Industrial Revolution gathered steam, and accelerated the migration of the population from country to city. The result of this movement was the development of horrifying slums and cramped row housing in the overcrowded cities. By 1900 AD 80% of the population lived in cities. These cities were organised into geographical zones based on social class. The poor in the inner city, with the more fortunate living further away from the city core. This was made possible by the development of suburban rail transit. Some suburban rail companies were required by law to provide cheap trains for workers to travel into the city centre…

Victorian Britain

Families in a Victorian street scene

Summary of Victorian Britain

The growth of rail transit also gave birth to that Victorian mainstay, the seaside resort. As the Industrial Revolution progressed, working hours decreased, and the introduction of Bank Holidays meant that workers had the time to take trips away from the cities to the seaside. The seaside resorts introduced the amusement pier to entertain visitors. Some of the more famous resorts were at Blackpool, Great Yarmouth and Brighton. The Industrial Revolution also meant that the balance of power shifted from the aristocracy, whose position and wealth was based on land, to the newly rich business leaders. The new aristocracy became one of wealth, not land, although titles, then as now, remained socially important in British society. There were railways of a sort before the 19th century in Britain. Tracks made of stone and iron carried wagons from mines and quarries under horse power. The invention of the steam engine changed things dramatically. Trevithick and Stephenson. In 1804 AD Richard Trevithick first harnessed a steam engine to a wagon. His engine was unsuccessful for transport, but the die was cast. Just a few years later George Stephenson's Rocket became the first steam locomotive practical to use for pulling rolling stock (train cars to you and me). Stephenson applied the new technology to his *Stockton and Darlington Railway* in 1825 AD, although in those early years horses still did some of the work…

Victorian Britain

A Victorian steam train

Summary of Victorian Britain

The L & M. The first truly successful steam railway was the *Liverpool and Manchester Railway* (1830 AD). The L&M sparked a feverish boom in railway building that lasted twenty years. By 1854 AD every town of any size in England was connected by rail, though Wales was less well served. One of the major problems of these early boom years was the lack of standardization (the same difficulty encountered by canal builders earlier). There were at least 5 different gauges (the distance between the rails) in use in the 1840's AD. This meant that trains made for one line could not use rails on another line, so goods would have to be unloaded and transferred to a new train of the proper gauge. This problem was not completely solved until the 1890's AD. Rail was the most popular means of transport for goods and people throughout the Victorian era and well into the 20th century. In a sense, rail set the tone for 19th century "progress" and made possible the entrepreneurial successes and excesses of the Industrial Revolution. Some prominent Victorian railway stations are still in use today, notably Paddington (the building, not the bear of the same name), St. Pancras, and York. Major rail museums also exist at Didcot and at York. After some pictures of life in Victorian Britain we will, in the next chapter, enter into Edwardian Britain…

Victorian Britain

A Victorian railway station

Victorians getting around the City

Victorian Britain

The Victorian seaside

A Victorian school room

Victorian Britain

A Victorian shop.

People outside their houses in Victorian times and now it is time for us to go into the Edwardian era…

Edwardian Britain

At the turn of the 19th century Great Britain was involved in the Second Boer War in South Africa and in 1901 AD Queen Victoria, who had reigned since 1837 AD, was succeeded by her son Edward VII, who, in turn, was succeeded by George V in 1910 AD. This period in Great Britain is called the Edwardian era. The Edwardian era or Edwardian period in the United Kingdom is the period covering the reign of King Edward VII, 1901 to 1910, and is sometimes extended beyond Edward's death to include years leading up to World War One. The death of Queen Victoria in January 1901 and the succession of her son Edward marked the end of the Victorian era…

Edwardian Britain

While Victoria had shunned society King Edward VII was part of a fashionable elite that liked to set the style and was influenced by the art and fashions of the day in Continental Europe which can perhaps be explained by the King's fondness for travel overseas. It was a time when Edwardian society had picnics in the park and generally had a nice life but this was not so true for the working classes...

Edwardian Britain

The era was marked by significant shifts in politics as sections of society that had been largely excluded from wielding power in the past, such as common labourers and women, became increasingly politicised.

The Edwardian period is frequently extended beyond King Edward's death in 1910 to include the years up to the sinking of the RMS *Titanic* in 1912, the start of World War I in 1914, the end of hostilities with Germany in 1918, or the signing of the Treaty of Versailles in 1919. After we have seen some pictures of the Edwardian period we will unfortunately march reluctantly into the dark days of The First World War…

Edwardian Britain

King Edward VII

Edwardian Britain

An Edwardian seaside

The Edwardian pier at Cromer in Norfolk

Edwardian Britain

Edwardian chums by the sea

Edwardian chums on the steps

Edwardian Britain

An Edwardian Post Office

Reading in an Edwardian parlour

Edwardian Britain

Tea outside an Edwardian house

The splendour of Edwardian buildings

Edwardian Britain

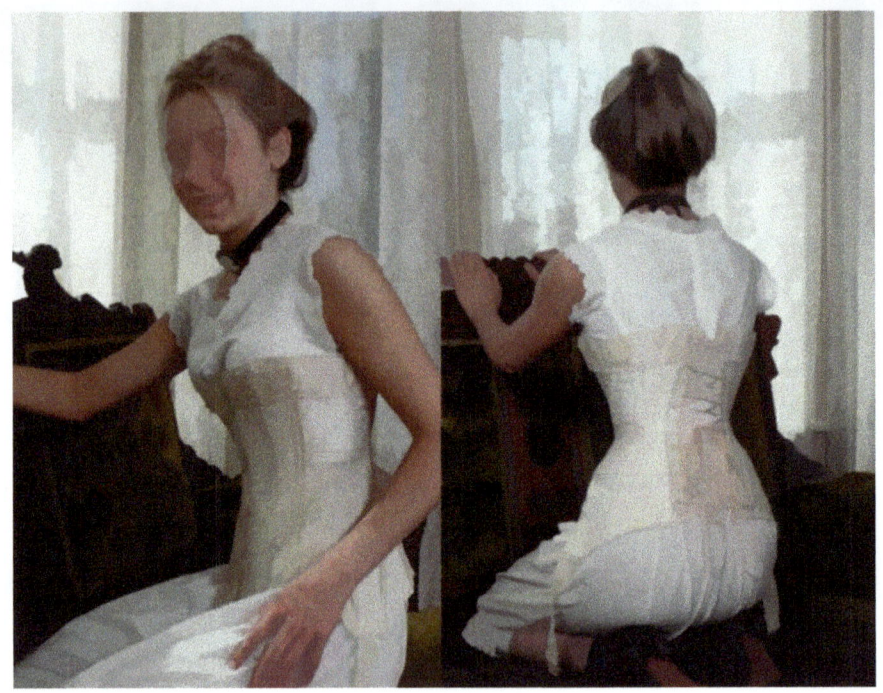

The beauty of the Edwardian under garments

An Edwardian cycle

Edwardian Britain

Edwardian's promenading by the sea

An Edwardian seaside resort

Edwardian Britain

An Edwardian peaceful front room

Edwardian gentlemen bravely strolling towards World War One…

The First World War

In 1914 AD, Britain entered the First World War by declaring war on Germany. Nearly a million Britons were killed in the war, which lasted until Germany's surrender on 11 November 1918 AD. The First World War of 1914–1918 period in the United Kingdom of Great Britain and Ireland then consisting of England, Scotland, Wales, and the whole of Ireland was one of the Allied Powers during the First World War of 1914–1918, fighting against the Central Powers (the German Empire, the Austro-Hungarian Empire, the Ottoman Empire and the Kingdom of Bulgaria…

The First World War

The British armed forces were increased in size largely because of the introduction in January 1916, of forced conscription for the first time in the kingdom's history as well as the raising of the largest all-volunteer army in history, known as Kitchener's Army, of more than two million men. The outbreak of war has generally been regarded as a socially unifying event, although this view has been challenged by more recent scholarship. In any case, responses in the United Kingdom in 1914 were similar to those amongst populations across Europe…

The First World War

The nations armed forces were reorganised and the war marked the creation of the Royal Air Force. On the eve of war, there was serious domestic unrest in the UK (amongst the labour and suffrage movements and especially in Ireland) but much of the population rapidly rallied behind the government. Significant sacrifices were made in the name of defeating the Empire's enemies and many of those who could not fight contributing to philanthropic and humanitarian causes. Fearing food shortages and labour shortfalls, the government passed legislation such as the Defence of the Realm Act, to give it new powers…

The First World War

The war saw a move away from the idea of "business as usual" under prime minister Herbert Henry Asquith and towards a state of total war (complete state intervention in public affairs) under David Lloyd George, the first time this had been seen in Britain. The war also witnessed the first aerial bombardments of cities in Britain. Newspapers played an important role in maintaining popular support for the war. Large quantities of propaganda were produced by the government…

The First World War

By adapting to the changing demographics of the workforce (or the "dilution of labour", as it was termed), war-related industries grew rapidly, and production increased, as concessions were quickly made to trade unions. In that regard, the war is also credited by some with drawing women into mainstream employment for the first time. Debates continue about the impact the war had on women's emancipation, given that a large number of women were granted the vote for the first time in 1918. The experience of individual women during the war varied; much depended on locality, age, marital status and occupation…

The First World War

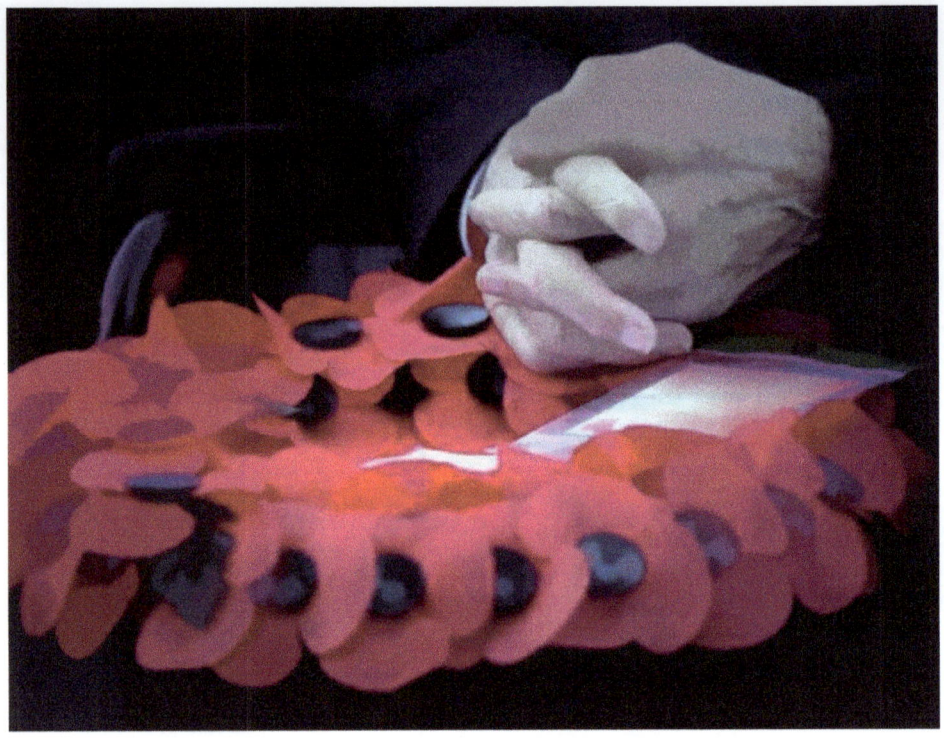

The civilian death rate rose due to food shortages and Spanish Flu, which hit the country in 1918. Military deaths are estimated to have exceeded 850,000.

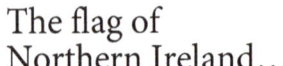
The flag of
Northern Ireland…

The Empire reached its zenith at the conclusion of peace negotiations. However, the war heightened not only imperial loyalties but also individual national identities in the dominions (Canada, Newfoundland, Australia, New Zealand, South Africa and India). Irish nationalists after 1916 moved from collaboration with London to demands for immediate independence, a move given great impetus by the Conscription Crisis of 1918…

The First World War

Field of red poppies

The Inter-war period was from 1919 to 1939: The inter-war period was the period between the end of World War I and the beginning of World War II. The period began with the Armistice with Germany that had concluded World War I in 1918 and following the Paris Peace Conference in 1919, and ending in 1939 with the invasion of Poland and the start of World War II. Home Rule in Ireland, which had been a major political issue since the late 19th century but put on hold by the war, was somewhat resolved after the Irish War of Independence brought the British Government to a stalemate and therefore, in 1922 AD. Negotiations led to the formation of the Irish Free State. However, in order to appease Unionists in the north, the north-eastern six counties remained as part of the U.K., with its own Parliament at Stormont in Belfast. Having been in power for much of the early 20th century under Prime Ministers Campbell-Bannerman, Asquith and Lloyd George the Liberal Party suffered a sharp decline from 1922 AD; the newly formed Labour Party, whose leader Ramsay Macdonald led two minority governments, swiftly became the Conservative's main opposition, and Britain's largest party of the left. King Edward VIII succeeded his father George V in January 1936 AD, but was quickly met with difficulties due to his love affair with Wallis Simpson. In December, he decided to abdicate in order to be able to marry Simpson, and his brother George VI was crowned King. Many believe that the First World War was stupid, tragic and futile. The stupidity of the war has been a theme of growing strength since the 1920's and the red poppy has become the national symbol for this futile waste of life…

The First World War

In the trenches

Waiting for the off

The First World War

Spying on the enemy

Waiting under Tower Bridge London

The First World War

Women of the Land Army working on the farm

The Land Army girls bring in the harvest

The First World War

Pedaling towards victory

Tank making in British factories

The First World War

World War One coin

Back on the home front

The First World War

Victorious British troops coming home only to be all to quickly returned once more to war just a few short years later. The dark clouds of the Second World War were looming and that is were we are marching straight onto next!…

The Second World War

The Second World War started when in order to avoid another European conflict, Prime Minister Neville Chamberlain attempted to appease German Chancellor Adolf Hitler, who was expanding his country's territory across Central Europe. Despite proclaiming that he has achieved "peace for our time", Britain declared war on Germany on 3 September 1939 AD, following Hitler's invasion of Poland two days earlier. When war was declared the U.K. thus joined the Allied Forces in opposition to the Axis forces of Nazi Germany and Fascist Italy. For the first time, civilians were not exempt from the war, as London suffered nightly bombings during the Blitz. At the war's end in 1945 AD, however, the U.K. emerged as one of the victorious nations. The Second World War of 1939 to 1945 saw Britain, along with most of its dominions, Crown Colonies, and British India, declared war on Nazi Germany in 1939. Many other nationalities joined forces with the UK. These included most of concurred Europe, Africa, and Asia and of course Russia and later on America. The war with Japan began in 1941, after it attacked British colonies in Asia…

The Second World War

Winston Churchill: Winston Churchill was born in 1874 into a wealthy and famous family. His father was Lord Randolph Churchill and he was the grandson of the 7th Duke of Marlborough. Winston Churchill was born at Blenheim Palace in Oxfordshire. He was schooled at Harrow where it is said that he only put his name on the exam entrance paper to get in. Churchill went to the Royal Military Academy at Sandhurst and gained a commission in the Fourth Hussars. He saw some military action and took part in the Battle of Omdurman in 1898. During the Boer War, he was a war correspondent. Winston Churchill was captured, held a prisoner, escaped and took part in the relief of Ladysmith. After this, Winston Churchill went into politics. He had a chequered career up World War Two and was seen as something of a maverick. In 1900, he was elected Conservative MP for Oldham but in 1904, he left the Conservative Party and joined the Liberal Party. From 1906 to 1908, he was a Liberal MP for northwest Manchester and from 1908 to 1922, he was an MP for Dundee. Between 1908 and 1910, Winston Churchill held a cabinet post President of the Board of Trade. In 1910, he was promoted to Home Secretary. As Home Secretary. From October 1911 to May 1915, Winston Churchill was made First Lord of the Admiralty. In this post, he did a great deal to ensure that the navy was in a state to fight a war. It was Winston Churchill was an early supporter of using planes in combat. However, Churchill was to pay the price for the bloody failure of the Dardanelles campaign in 1915. It was Winston Churchill who proposed the expedition to the War Council and, as a result, he was held responsible for its failure. He was dismissed from his post at the Admiralty and he was made Chancellor of the Duchy of Lancaster. Having been Home Secretary and First Lord at the Admiralty, this was seen by many, including Winston Churchill, to be a demotion and he left the post after just six months. Churchill then re-joined the army…

The Second World War

Winston Churchill: Winston Churchill quickly returned to government. In 1917 he was appointed Minister for Munitions. It was a post he held until 1918. In 1919, Winston Churchill was appointed Minister for War and Air. A post he held until 1920. In 1921, he was appointed Colonial Secretary. A post he held until he lost his seat for Dundee in the 1922 election. He became MP for Epping in 1924 standing as a 'constitutional anti-socialist'. Stanley Baldwin, leader of the Conservative Party, appointed him to the post of the Chancellor of the Exchequer and Winston Churchill officially re-joined the Conservative Party in 1925. Churchill remained outside of government from 1929 to 1939. As Hitler became more and more aggressive in Europe, Winston Churchill became more and more concerned about the stance taken by the then leader of the government, Neville Chamberlain. From 1938 to the outbreak of war in September 1939, Churchill urged the government to be more pro-active against Adolf Hitler, including for an early call for conscription. On September 3rd, 1939, Winston Churchill was back in the government when Chamberlain appointed him First Lord of the Admiralty. On May 10th, 1940, Winston Churchill became Prime Minister and during the Second World War, he was the most dominant figure in British politics. A role, that he received huge praise for once the war was over. To many people in Britain, Churchill's stand against Nazism and all it stood for, summarised why the war was being fought. His speeches have become part of legend be it 'fighting on the beaches' or his salute to the men from Fighter Command who took on the Luftwaffe in the Battle of Britain "Never in the field of human conflict has so much been owed by so many to so few". One of the things that endeared him to the people of London and the wider UK was that Churchill remained in London during the Blitz and he regularly visited areas bombed out by the Luftwaffe. To the people of London, he was one of them and a man who could have removed himself from the dangers of German bombers, but refused to, staying in bombed out London along with those who suffered…

The Second World War

Winston Churchill: Churchill also took a role in military issues. It was he who was the political force behind the creation of commando units that would be sent in to disrupt the German military. He was also scathing about military defeats, calling the defeat at Tobruk a "disgrace". During the war, Winston Churchill also held a number of meetings with other wartime leaders. He met F.D.Roosevelt, the American president, on nine occasions between 1941 and 1945; he had five meetings with the Russian leader Stalin between 1942 and 1945. For all his popularity as a war leader, Winston Churchill lost the 1945 general election to Labour's Clement Atlee. His wife told him that it might be a 'blessing in disguise'. Winston Churchill is said to have replied that it was 'very well disguised'. In October 1951, he became Prime Minister once again. However, Churchill had suffered a stroke in August 1949 that had been kept secret from the public and his health was now a concern. Aged 77 in 1951, Winston Churchill was not in a fit enough state to involve himself in day-to-day politics as required from a Prime Minister. In April 1953, he was made a Knight of the Garter and he resigned from politics in 1955. However, few people could match his international status. Having won a Nobel Prize for Literature in 1953, he became an honorary American citizen in 1963. An honour confirmed by Congress. Winston Churchill died in 1965 and was buried less than one mile from where he was born at Blenheim Palace. For many people, his stubborn refusal to admit defeat or that it was a lost cause during World War Two has given him a deserved reputation few other politicians have ever achieved…

The Second World War

A significant event of the Second World War was the bombing of British cities such as the London blitz and the near destruction of Coventry, Hull and other major UK cites. In the above artwork we see St Paul's Cathedral surrounded by blitz smoke and bombed out buildings. It is a testament to the skills and hard work of the London Fire Brigade assisted by the general public that this building escaped largely undamaged and can be visited today. While Great Britain faced bombing raids our brave airmen of the R.A.F fought for our very existence in the sky. The battle of Britain that took part in the skies above Britain prompted Winston Churchill to broadcast his famous speech: "Never in the field of human conflict has so much been owed by so many to so few".

The turning point of the Second World War was undoubtedly seen on the 6th June 1944 when the allies launched a massive assault on the Normandy beaches. This was called D-Day. The allied troops had prepared for ages and just needed the right weather conditions to launch what was the biggest sea borne invasion and the greatest military campaign the world has ever seen…

The Second World War

The Axis Powers were defeated by the Allies in 1945 and again Winston Churchill went on the radio at 3 pm on the 8th May 1945 to tell his people that victory in Europe had been achieved and that the nation could have a day's national holiday to celebrate VE Day…

The Second World War

Victory over Japan Day (also known as Victory in the Pacific Day, V-J Day, or V-P Day) is a name chosen for the day on which Japan surrendered, which in effect ended World War II. Japan's surrender was made on the afternoon of August 15, 1945, in Japan. August 15th is the official V-J Day for the UK, while the official U.S. commemoration is September 2nd…

The Second World War

War is Declared

English airmen scramble as the alarm is sounded

The Second World War

Tanks mobilise in the desert of Africa

German fighter plane in the sky above London during the blitz

The Second World War

Battle of Britain fighters take to the air (Spitfires)

Practicing for D-Day

The Second World War

Planting Anderson shelters into their back gardens

A Spitfire in the skies above the English countryside

The Second World War

Gas Masks at the Ready

American fighter plane

The Second World War

Lady welders working in a factory during the war

Pilots ready for the OFF

The Second World War

Londoners off to the air raid shelter

Children playing on a London bomb site

The Second World War

A Nazi flag

Londoners sheltering from the blitz in the London underground

The Second World War

Always time for a cup of tea mate!

American bomber

The Second World War

Children leaving their parents in the Cities and Towns to go and live in the countryside

After the war finished people were housed in temporary housing but until they were built children were sent out into the countryside to live safe from the blitz while their parents stayed behind in the bombed out cities…

The Second World War

People celebrating Victory in Europe Day with flags and bunting which was the beginning of the end of World War Two. Next we will enter into the Post War Years which although rationing continued after the war for several years things did begin to get better.

For me personally things got even better in 1949 when I was born and I was able to commence my own journey through history that has eventually led me to wanting to discover where I came from and hence ultimately to this book. In our last chapter we head into the brave new world of Post War Britain…

Post War Britain - Great Britain from 1945 to 2019

In 1945 much re-building was required in Great Britain

Great Britain from 1945 to 2019

Britain was a victor in World War II and its people settled down to enjoy post war peace in the hope of better things to come!…

Post War Britain - Great Britain from 1945 to 2019

Great Britain gave independence to India in 1947 and gave up nearly all of the rest of the Empire by 1970, finally it ended in 1997 with the handover of Hong Kong to China. Britain was a founding member of the United Nations in 1945, with a veto in the Security Council…

Post War Britain - Great Britain from 1945 to 2019

The Flags of England, Scotland, Wales and Northern Ireland flying high

Great Britain collaborated closely with the United States during the Cold War after 1947, and in 1949 helped form NATO as a military alliance against the Soviet Union. Britain fought North Korea and China in the Korean War from 1950 to 1953. After a long debate and initial rejection, Britain joined the European Economic Community (EEC) in 1973. Prosperity returned in the 1950's and London remained a world centre for finance and culture, but the nation is no longer a major world power…

Post War Britain - Great Britain from 1945 to 2019

In Post War Britain rationing and queuing was still the norm for many/everyone for several more years

Winston Churchill, who had been leader of the wartime coalition government, suffered a surprising landslide defeat to Clement Attlee's Labour party in 1945 elections. Attlee created the Welfare State in Britain, which most notably provided free healthcare under the National Health Service. By the late 1940's, the Cold War was underway, which would dominate British foreign policy for another 40 years. In 1951, Churchill and the Tories returned to power; they would govern uninterrupted for the next 13 years. King George VI died in 1952, and was succeeded by his eldest daughter, Elizabeth II our current Queen. Churchill was succeeded in 1955 by Sir Anthony Eden, whose premiership was dominated by the Suez Crisis, in which Britain, France and Israel plotted to bomb Egypt after its President Nasser nationalised the Suez Canal…

Post War Britain - Great Britain from 1945 to 2019

Prefabricated houses were being put up just after the war and in some places they are still in use to this very day

Sir Anthony Eden's successor, Harold Macmillan, split the Conservatives when Britain applied to join the European Economic Community, but French President Charles de Gaulle vetoed the application. Labour returned to power in 1964 under Harold Wilson, who brought in a number of social reforms, including the legalisation of abortion, the abolition of capital punishment and the decriminalisation of homosexuality. Harold Wilson, having lost the 1970 election to Edward Heath, returned to power in 1974; however, Labour's reputation was harmed by the Winter of Discontent of 1978-9 under Jim Callaghan, which enabled the Conservatives to re-take control of Parliament in 1979, under the leadership of Margaret Thatcher, Britain's first female Prime Minister. Although Margaret Thatcher's economic reforms made her initially unpopular, her decision in 1982 to retake the Falkland Islands from invading Argentine forces, in what would become known as the Falklands War, changed her fortunes and enabled a landslide election victory in 1983. After winning an unprecedented third election in 1987, however, Thatcher's popularity began to fade and she was replaced by former chancellor John Major in 1990. Tensions between Protestants and Catholics in Northern Ireland came to a head in the late 1960's, when nationalist participants in a civil rights march were shot by members of the B Specials, a reserve police force manned almost exclusively by unionists. From this point the Provisional Irish Republican Army, also known as the Provos or simply the IRA, began a bombing campaign throughout the U.K., beginning a period known as The Troubles, which lasted until the late 1990's…

Post War Britain - Great Britain from 1945 to 2019

Lady window cleaners in the 1930's

Prince Charles the Prince of Wales and Elizabeth's eldest son married Lady Diana Spencer in 1981; the couple had two children, William and Harry, but divorced in 1992, during which year Prince Andrew and Princess Anne also separated from their spouses, leading the Queen to call the year her "annus horribilis". In 1997, Diana was killed in a car crash in Paris, leading to a mass outpouring of grief across the United Kingdom, and indeed the world. On the international stage, the second half of the 20th century was dominated by the Cold War between the Soviet Union and its socialist allies and the United States and its capitalist allies; the U.K. was a key supporter of the latter, joining the anti-Soviet military alliance NATO in 1949 (the year that I was born). In this period, the U.K. became involved in several Cold War conflicts, such as the Korean War (1950–1953). In contrast, the Republic of Ireland remained neutral and provided troops to U.N. peacekeeping missions. In 1997, Tony Blair was elected prime minister in a landslide victory for the so-called "New Labour", economically following the "Third Way". Blair won re-election in 2001 and 2005, before handing over power to his chancellor Gordon Brown in 2007. After a decade of prosperity both the U.K. and the Irish Republic were affected by the global recession, which began in 2008. In 2010, the Conservative party formed a coalition government with the Liberal Democrats, with Tory leader David Cameron as Prime Minister. In 2015 David Cameron won a majority for the Conservative party. He is no longer the Prime Minister and was replaced by Teresa May in 2016. In May of 2019 she decided she would stand down in June 2019. The Conservatives only have a slim majority at the moment but are still in power as I write awaiting a new leader!…

Post War Britain - Great Britain from 1945 to 2019

The Police still directed the traffic in the 1950's and factory workers all went to work on their bikes at the time

Modern Great Britain

The concept of the modern world as distinct from an ancient or medieval world rests on a sense that the modern world is not just another era in history, but rather the result of a new type of change. This is usually conceived of as progress driven by deliberate human efforts to better their situation. I feel very fortunate to have been born and to have lived in modern Great Britain. It has enabled me to travel, not just in the UK but abroad, and meet, see and marvel at all that our modern world has to offer…

Post War Britain - Great Britain from 1945 to 2019

Famous People of the Modern Era in Great Britain

Baroness Margaret Thatcher: Baroness Margaret Thatcher, the 'Iron Lady', was the first female British Prime Minister and the longest serving PM for over 150 years. Margaret Thatcher's father, a shopkeeper and Mayor of Grantham, was a major influence in her childhood. She was educated at the local grammar school and she went on to studied Chemistry at Oxford University, where she became president of the university Conservative association. Margaret Thatcher was elected as the Conservative MP for Finchley in 1959. She held junior posts before becoming Shadow Spokesperson for Education, and entered the Cabinet as Education Secretary in 1970. In Opposition she then stood against Edward Heath for the party leadership in 1975 and won. In 1979, the Conservative Party won the General Election and Margaret Thatcher became PM. Her first 2 years in office were not easy, unemployment was very high, but the economy gradually showed improvement. She added to her reputation by leading the country to war against Argentina in the Falkland Islands. The Conservatives went on to win the 1983 election by an overwhelming majority, helped by a divided opposition. Her government followed a radical programme of privatisation and deregulation, reform of the trade unions, tax cuts and the introduction of market mechanisms into health and education. One great difficulty during her time in office was the issue of Europe. Her long-serving Foreign Secretary, Sir Geoffrey Howe resigned in November 1990 in protest at her attitude to Europe. Michael Heseltine challenged her for the leadership, and while he failed to win, he gained 152 votes which was enough to make it evident that a crucial minority wanted a change. Thatcher was eventually persuaded not to go forward to the second ballot, which was then won by her Chancellor of the Exchequer, John Major. She left the House of Commons in 1992, and was appointed a life peerage in the House of Lords in the same year, receiving the title of Baroness Thatcher of Kesteven. In 1995 she was appointed as Lady Companion of the Order of the Garter, the highest order of Chivalry in the UK. Margaret Thatcher died on 8 April 2013 at The Ritz Hotel in London, after suffering a stroke. She received a ceremonial funeral including full military honours, with a church service at St Paul's Cathedral...

Post War Britain - Great Britain from 1945 to 2019

Today in Modern Great Britain

The United Kingdom become an issue when in the 2000's Scotland voting as to whether they would stayed in the union or leave. Thankfully, I believe, they voted to stay part of the United Kingdom. In 2016 the then Prime Minister of Great Britain David Cameron re-negotiated the terms of Great Britain remaining within the EU. The people of the United Kingdom then voted as to whether we remain within the EU or go our own way in June 2016. Personally Susie and I voted to remain in the EU with our European cousins however, a small majority of our citizens voted to leave so we are due to leave on or before April 2019. As I have already mentioned the people of the UK voted to leave so David Cameron resigned as Prime Minister and was replaced by Teresa May. We should have left the EU at the end of April 2019 however the politicians could not agree the way forward and to date we are now scheduled to leave in October 2019. Teresa May tried her best to get the agreement of Parliament to her planned withdrawal bill but she failed on more than one occasion. In May 2019 Teresa May decided enough was enough and she was going to step down. So far there has been ten candidates who have put their name forward to become the new Prime Minister. Some on each side of the argument so who knows what will happen next! As I am putting the finishing touches to this book we still await an outcome! While we wait here are some pictures of post war Great Britain between 1945 and 2019 for your enjoyment before I stop typing and finally finish this book!…

Post War Britain - Great Britain from 1945 to 2019

The classic British Telecommunications Telephone of the 1940's

Smoggy day in London in the 1950's

Post War Britain - Great Britain from 1945 to 2019

Truck of the 1940's

Beach wear of the 1950's

Post War Britain - Great Britain from 1945 to 2019

Ladies fashion in the 1940's

Helping Mum in the 1940's. I can still remember helping my Mum by turning our mangle handle even in the late 50's…

Post War Britain - Great Britain from 1945 to 2019

Train station in Yorkshire in the 1940's

Hair styles of the 1940's

Post War Britain - Great Britain from 1945 to 2019

The War Memorial Flight taking to the air in the 1950's

Girls at play in the 1950's

Post War Britain - Great Britain from 1945 to 2019

Radio of the 1950's

Convenience food started to become more readily available in the 1950's

Post War Britain - Great Britain from 1945 to 2019

Coach travel in the 1950's

Norwich Stars Speedway racing in the 1950's. I went several times in the 60's with my mates and enjoyed it very much but sadly the stadium was sold and pulled down. The team moved to Kings Lynn which is very close to where I live today!…

Post War Britain - Great Britain from 1945 to 2019

Neighbours chatting over the fence in the 1950's.

People in a Norwich record shop in the 1960's

Post War Britain - Great Britain from 1945 to 2019

Children doing their homework with mum in the 1960's

The Mini Skirt in the 1960's

Post War Britain - Great Britain from 1945 to 2019

People in the 1960's started to take more, and more seaside holidays

Teenage's began to become more visible in the 1960's (I was at various times a mod and a skin head) Oh happy days!

Post War Britain - Great Britain from 1945 to 2019

The 1960's was the dawn of the scooter age. I had a Vespa of my own as a young teenager and I love my Vespa very, very much

The flags of all the EU member countries in 2016

Post War Britain - Great Britain from 1945 to 2019

The Skin Heads of the 1970's. I was one during my teenage years

Although, the Scottish girls, had long stopped coming to Great Yarmouth, to fillet the herring fish catch, by the mid-50's, other things had moved on as well. Great Britain joined the EU in the 70's. Prime Minister Margaret Thatcher, who was elected in the 1970's became, some would say, along with Winston Churchill, one of the greatest leaders, that Great Britain has ever known. We will finish our picture extravaganza by seeing some more pictures showcasing some of the beautiful views of Great Britain today and some of my watercolour paintings…

Post War Britain - Great Britain from 1945 to 2019

The Houses of Parliament

The Lake District…

Post War Britain - Great Britain from 1945 to 2019

Flying!

More Flying!

Post War Britain - Great Britain from 1945 to 2019

Mousehole harbour in Cornwall.

Down the road to Glencoe

Post War Britain - Great Britain from 1945 to 2019

Mousehole harbour in Cornwall

Highlander

Post War Britain - Great Britain from 1945 to 2019

Norfolk Bluebell woods

Walking on Brighton Pier

Post War Britain - Great Britain from 1945 to 2019

Poppy in Shouldham Warren on lookout in 2019

Charlie in our Norfolk garden in 2018

Post War Britain - Great Britain from 1945 to 2019

Alan, Ginny, Lou, Gerard and Olivia on Wells beach in Norfolk

Norwich market stall

Post War Britain - Great Britain from 1945 to 2019

Boats in Mousehole harbour in Cornwall

Norwich City FC players celebrating promotion back to the premiership in 2015 and then again in May 2019 with their fans, of which I am proud to be one. I hope there is much more success for my team in the years ahead...

Post War Britain - Great Britain from 1945 to 2019

We finish our journey with a Union Jack which is the symbol of this great country that is called England which is part of Great Britain and the nation that is called the United Kingdom.

As we reach the end of our journey together, have I answered my question: Where do I come from? Well I think I have. I come from a people that have lived on this island since the age of man begun. We have developed our culture, beliefs and skills from the movement and inter-breading of many different peoples from all over Europe and beyond. So I come from the wider world and I believe the people of England are all the better for it. In this book I have taken a personal and selective exploration into the history of where I come from and therefore, the content for you may well vary considerably dependant on where you come from and what aspects of your history appeals to you. So I hope you have enjoyed our journey through the history of England together and I hope that it may inspire others to research their own origins and heritage. So until we meet again, have a great life, enjoy living and always be proud of who you are and where you come from. Remember we are ALL part of the same family of human beings! …

Acknowledgement

I would like to thank all the people that I have met during my long and happy lifetime. They have enriched my life and the enjoyment of living in England immeasurably . I would also like to thank my publishers Rainbow Publications UK. For publishing this book and for giving me the opportunity for my words to be read once more. Finally I wish to thank my wife Susie for all her love and support she gives me in all that I do every day of my life.

Susie… 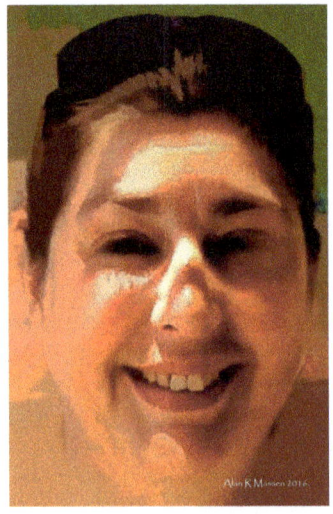  …Alan

Copyright © 2019 Alan R. Massen

I wish you all a very special

Thank You

www.ingramcontent.com/pod-product-compliance
Lightning Source LLC
Chambersburg PA
CBHW061927290426

44113CB00024B/2832